# Art, Misuse and Technology:

# Micheál O'Connell's 'System Interference'

**John Roberts**

**Uillinn: West Cork Arts Centre, 2022**

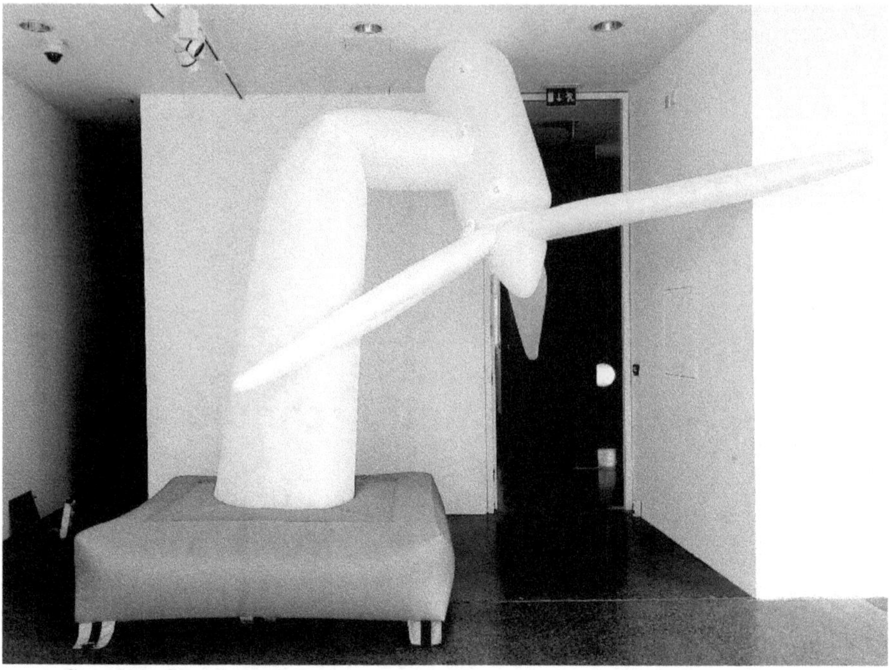
*Inflated/Deflated Wind Turbine* 1 of 2. Photo by Micheál O'Connell, 2022

# Art, Misuse and Technology:

# Micheál O'Connell's 'System Interference'

John Roberts

Uillinn: West Cork Arts Centre, 2022

This book has been published by West Cork Arts Centre on the occasion of Micheál O'Connell / Mocksim's touring exhibition *System Interference*

Uillinn: West Cork Arts Centre, Skibbereen
17 September to 26 October 2022

Wexford Arts Centre
21 August to 5 October 2023

Highlanes Gallery, Drogheda
25 November 2023 to 17 February 2024

Micheál O'Connell was awarded a *Visual Art Commissions Award* to produce new work by The Arts Council / An Chomhairle Ealaíon, 2020, and the exhibitions are supported by *Touring and Dissemination of Work Scheme* funding, 2022.

Author: Roberts, John
Title: Art, Misuse, and Technology: Micheál O'Connell's 'System Interference'
ISBN-10 1-904354-39-4, ISBN-13: 978-1-90-435439-0 (hardback)


the arts council an chomhairle ealaíon 70 YEARS

UILLINN WEST CORK ARTS CENTRE

wexfordartscentre ARTS FOR ALL, ARTS FOR LIFE

Hlg Highlanes Gallery

Comhairle Contae Chorcaí
Cork County Council

Cover image, *Artificial Stupidity*, Micheál O'Connell

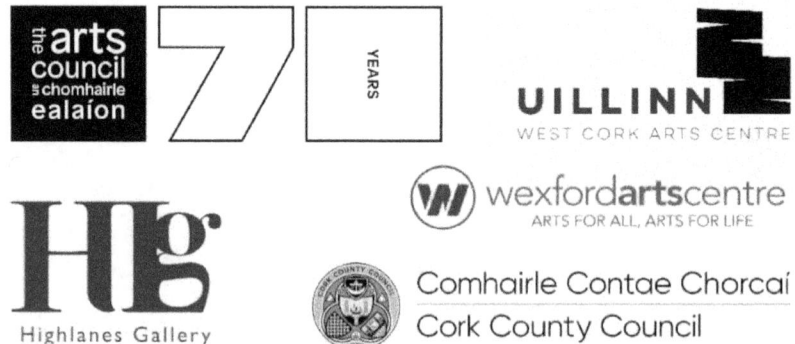

## Foreword

Uillinn: West Cork Arts Centre is delighted to present System Interference, a solo exhibition of new and recent work by Micheál O'Connell / Mocksim. Appropriation and unearthing the poetic in everyday, often dysfunctional, technologies, systems and bureaucracies are key to his activities. I became acquainted with his 'systems interference' approach while he completed a two-month residency at Uillinn in 2019 where he participated in the cultural life of the area, ran several events, maintained focus on his technological interests and produced new work.

An Arts Council Commissions Award in 2020 enabled a period of research and development from 2020 to 2022, when Micheál spent blocks of time in residence at Uillinn, strengthening links with practitioners and artists locally, exploring his ideas and concerns, and investigating found/ready-made objects and materials.

Writer and philosopher John Roberts, who is Professor of Art and Aesthetics at the University of Wolverhampton, has been observing the process from the beginning. His theorising and writing on the social ontology of photography, avant-garde and conceptual art history, and on the political implications of institutional, extra-institutional and socially engaged practices, inform Micheál's understanding of the place of art, or 'post-art art', today.

John's papers and books, including *The Necessity of Errors*, 'Trickster', and *The Philistine Controversy* (co-authored with Dave Beech), are relevant to aspects of Micheál's 'systems interference' practice. It has been a privilege to have him involved with the project, and I give enormous thanks to John for his perceptive, illuminating and substantial text. Thanks also to Marc Beishon, science reporter and editor, for his informed and thorough proofreading of the final text.

System Interference has also received an Arts Council Touring and Dissemination of Work Scheme award that will enable it to tour to Wexford Arts Centre, and Highlanes Gallery, Drogheda, in 2023. I would like to thank Catherine Bowe, Visual Art Curator at Wexford Arts Centre, and Aoife Ruane, Director of Highlanes Gallery for so enthusiastically embracing this project.

I wish to thank our public whose support for Uillinn allows us to push artistic boundaries and create challenging experiences. I also wish to thank the ongoing support of The Arts Council / An Chomhairle Ealaíon, Cork County Council and the Department of Social Protection.

Thanks to the team at Uillinn for their unwavering hard work and commitment – Stephen Canty, Justine Foster, Louise Forsyth, Kate McElroy, Sarah Canty, Jackie O'Callaghan, Gavin Buckley, Claire Lambert, Gráinne Capels and Piotr Lickiewicz, as well as the West Cork Arts Centre Board for their steadfast support of Micheál O'Connell's work and the ongoing work of the Centre.

Above all I give my sincere thanks to Micheál for being so generous in his thinking, time and energy in the making of this exhibition, the associated programme of events and this publication. It has been a great pleasure working on this project with Micheál and I look forward to its continuing development as the exhibition tours to the other venues, contexts and communities.

Ann Davoren
Director
Uillinn: West Cork Arts Centre

**Acknowledgements**

Thanks to Chris and Paul for their good advice, to Laura for love and good humour, to Micheál for the uplifts and downdraughts of 'intelligent stupidity', and to my daughter Gilda, for everything.

## Contents

# Art, Misuse and Technology

Micheál O'Connell (a.k.a. Mocksim)[1] once pursued ambitions as a stand-up comedian, with serious intentions to play the Irishman-in-London as a whimsical Irish card. But, as with these things, the Irishness soon edged into the Oirish and paddywhackery as British audiences wanted the comedy comfortable and familiar, not exactly the Plain People of Ireland, in Flann O'Brien's immortal phrase, but rather, more the likable daftness and stupefaction of the idiot savant or feminized male ingénue, so beautifully cultivated by Ardal O'Hanlon as Father Dougal McGuire in the Channel 4 TV show *Father Ted* (1995–1998). In submitting to this, O'Connell felt there was only limited scope for subversion in jokes, tales, and wry observation from the 'green', before the audiences wanted you to play it just like the gormless stereotype. For a while, however, he took the comedy very seriously, even being offered representation by the management of Stewart Lee (Avalon) and achieving a place in the finals of the Amused Moose National Talent contest along with Simon Amstell and Rhod Gilbert. The initial passion was indeed highly focused and was largely to do with his then desire to escape his successful career as a high-level visualization programmer, as part of a global Modelling and Simulation team whose clients included Telecom Italia Mobile and Williams, Formula 1. The comedy allowed him to churn up all the attachments of a corporate-tech career that had increasingly threatened to suppress his political commitments – which had, only a few years before, driven and defined his life as a full-time organizer for the Trotskyist group, Militant, when he led a campaign to stop the closure of Charing Cross Hospital and organized a successful rent strike on South Acton Estate in London. But if the comedy led him out of a corporate life, the politics led him to make the comedic work in a different way after stand-up

[1] Mocksim: (Moc are the artist's initials; sim stands for simulation, as in 'modelling reality'; and 'k' stands semantically for 'mockery').

through his switch to the study of fine art. After completing a master's degree in fine art at the University of Brighton in 2006, it became clearer to him that in the period of art's formal and cognitive expansion after the deepening crisis of art's medium specificity in the 1990s, the expanded multidisciplinary space of art offered no fears and worries regarding the compatibility between the comedic, politics, tech-skills, system analysis and the performative. Indeed, what might be made from these encounters could, invitingly, provide a further critical re-assessment of the identity of the artist and artistic skill in a period of increasing flux and volatility for art after modernism and postmodernism. Interlinking comedy and the performative to his tech-skills offered a set of positions and strategies that were able to produce something interestingly hands-on for artistic practice: an actual politics of *technē* and technology in art in a period of increasing digitalized social control and surveillance. In fact, this technical refocusing of art and technology for O'Connell was a political response to a wider generational problem for artists in the new millennium in the wake of 'art after art in the expanded field': how to use, understand, work with, work against, technology with the rise of the internet and platform capitalism in a sceptical way that was more than simply late-Romantic anti-technologism. The encounter between art and technology had to have cultural ramifications other than mere aesthetic negation or apocalyptic fear or, conversely, its neutral appropriation. For without breaking with the lure and would-be self-evident rationalizations of technology, without testing its logical claims, the functions of technology easily slip back into dominant deterministic modes. That is, art's encounter had to establish a critique of technology that developed a working relationship with its logic of calculability and affects; thereby transposing what the artist did more precisely *with* technology – where he or she stood practically and immanently in relation to its systematic organizing power in the ongoing epoch of its political economic expansion and coercions and the vast technical extension (and diminishment) of human capacities and skills. The millennial artist has had to think catachrestically both inside and outside of neoliberalism's technology-as-system to *unthink* technology's capitalist naturalization.

## Chapter 1: Catastrophe and Efficiency

The artist's relationship to technology has been crucial to the mediation of the threat and proclaimed technical progress of capitalist modernity in European and North and South American culture since the beginning of the 20th century; just as the comedic and the sardonic have played a key part in the initial critical encounter with this technology's social and productive power, across both art and literature. Marcel Duchamp's *Fountain* (1917), and the *Bride Stripped Bare by Her Bachelors, Even* [*The Large Glass*] (1915–1923), and Francis Picabia's *Universal Prostitution* (*Prostitution Universelle*) (1917) and *Amorous Parade* (*Parade Amoureuse* (1917), for instance provide a range of the first visual conceptualizations of a world in which technology appears not only to have abstractly refunctioned the meaning of artistic and productive labour (*Fountain*), but the labour of (heterosexual) human relations as well. In *Universal Prostitution* and *Amorous Parade*, the relationships between men and women are reduced to the calculable operations of mechanical parts. In *Amorous Parade*, for example, Picabia presents a tableau of linked machinic parts/objects non-naturalistically (flat to the picture plane) inside a cold, off-white interior with scruffy grey marks, that may or may not mimic the look of marble veins. On the right of the space a spark plug-like object extends from a green drum, the tip of which is attached to a flywheel inside an open fronted box, and on top of which is placed what appears to be a flue shaped like a sports megaphone. Attached to the left side of the spark plug is a five-jointed black mechanical arm that is linked on the left of the space to a stanchion which below splits, like a tuning fork, into two feet that thicken into tubes extending into a bar on which are drawn two circles (presumably ovaries). The internal relations between abstracted male and female sexual parts reveal an alienated perfunctoriness that produces, overall, a deflated sense of discrepancy between the efficiency, calculability, and the would-be advance of reason, reflective of the new urbanity and modernity and fleshly pleasure. This visualization of technology as alienated machinic intercession – the substitution of body parts and bodily relations with machinic parts and relations – haunts this initial moment of the modernist internalization of industrialized technological adaptation. Technology appears, certainly in Picabia's work (less the case in Duchamp's early 'readymades', which are directly attuned to the role of technology in the rise of abstract labour), as an evasive, abstract, superfluous erosion of human efficacy, a cruel forcing and imposition. But it is more crucially the capitalist-military state's industrial development of technology that pushes this sense of 'technological forcing' into a far more urgent and threatening register here. For despite the relative charm of these machine-part pictures – their nod aesthetically to a certain notion of delicate ingenuity – they are also obliquely war pictures (a new world of machinic confrontation and military prosthetics) and pictures of a newly emergent administrative calculability: the scientific management of the office and the rise of a modern, technological bureaucracy. The technological threat here is not just obviously violent but dehumanizing and deindividuating; body parts as machine parts are subject to rigid external organization.

Indeed, human-technology duality in this period is shaped by two overdetermining categories: technology as violent trauma, as a result of the shattering consequences of imperialism and the Great War and the militarization of the European economy, and the further erosion of artisanal and manual skills through the technological reorganization of labour in the factory and office (Taylorism), through the greater collective systematization of human agency and knowledge – what Marx called the reduction of 'complex labour' to 'simple labour'. It is no surprise, therefore, that technology and its rationalistic administrative outcomes in this period define human action, labour power and cognitive capacity in highly reduced terms, diminishing human freedom and creativity through the submission of the worker and citizen to external systems and the seemingly arbitrary effects of administrative fiat or indifference. This is highly defined in literature. We see this expressly in Franz Kafka's *The Trial* (*Der Process*) (written 1915, published 1925),[2] a metaphysically and hypertrophic charged version of this new world of technologically efficient bureaucracy, and in Hans Fallada's pre-Nazi *Little Man, What Now?* (*Kleiner Mann – was nun?*) (1932)[3] – the story of destroyed opportunities and narrowed horizons under Great Depression conditions (unemployment had risen from 1.4 million to 6 million in Germany from 1929), as older forms of labour skill become superfluous to the technological reorganization of mass production. As such, Fallada's anti-hero, Johannes Pinneberg, is the discarded and imperilled 'new worker' of this conjunction, one of the growing army of new white collar workers who, atomized by the new employment conditions and growth in non-manual labour, are caught between feelings of class superiority regarding ordinary proletarian life, and an inexorable sense of powerlessness and anxiety about retail store employment and office life, in the face of the increasing technological rationalization and streamlining of business administration and state bureaucracy. That is, the new department store worker and the new office worker feel no less subject to disciplinary speed-ups and time and motion studies than the factory worker, but without any compensatory sense of class solidarity in the workplace, making the office worker and shop worker susceptible, as implied in Fallada's narrative, to the *ressentiment* of authoritarianism and fascism. These new conditions and increasing sense of class displacement for the new office worker and shop worker are explored in Siegfried Kracauer's path-breaking, *The Salaried Masses: Duty and Distraction in Weimar Germany* (*Die Angestellten: Aus dem neuesten Deutschland)* (1930), which was the first major analysis of the impact of these changes in class relations,

---

[2] Franz Kafka, *The Trial*, Penguin Classics, London, 2019

[3] Hans Fallada, *Little Man – What Now?*, Melville House, New York, 2009

highlighting how inescapable the interface between, technology and labour efficiency had become during the Great Depression.[4]

The identification of these new disciplinary structures, then, serves a particularly imaginary role in the art and literature of the time: factory and office work defined an urban world and a world of modernity as one in which order and systematization produces a monstrous excess of purposeless efficiency. If technology has the power of extending the violence of the state, it also has the capacity for creating pointless forms of market rationalization that benefit only owners and overseers. Thus, the idea that worker adaptation to new forms of technology and rational administration was part of a great new experiment in rational prosperity for all was to reveal how actually limited was the concept of bourgeois progress. This is why during the 1920s and 1930s humour and the comedic played such a crucial part in modernism's mediation of the human-technology duality. For it is humour above all in this period that is popularly perceived as a vivid means of destabilizing the logic of enforced and coercive rationalization and, as such, is best suited artistically to deflating the imperiousness of technological progress. Irony, inversion, exaggeration, mockery are able to expose the presumptuousness of rational efficiency and technological progress through showing up what is perceived to be the clear benefits of the rational and ordered, as opposed to the rational and ordered being simply evidence of the inflexible and instrumental. Laughter and amusement are invariably produced through highlighting the overweening rational perfectionism attached to system building.

Henri Bergson at the very beginning of these processes of industrial rationalization was the first to understand this modern link between laughter and the presumptions of rational efficiency. In 1900 he published *Laughter: An Essay on the Meaning of the Comic* (*Le Rire: Essai sur la signification du comique*) that demonstrated first

[4] Siegfried Kracauer, *The Salaried Masses: Duty and Distraction in Weimar Germany*, Verso, London and New York, 1998

and foremost how much of the modern experience of comedy derives from exposing the hubris of technology and industrial rationality, given the increasing powerlessness that workers and citizens felt in the new world of inventories, timetables, and production lines.[5] Blind to the failures of rationalization, given its indifference to human capacity, the modern machine or administrative system that works on regardless, unresponsive to any user feedback, is funny and maladroit. The human inability to keep up, navigate and adjust, therefore becomes a comedic deflation of these expectations, a recognition of how much the machinic rationalization of work practices and outcomes defeats, exhausts and diminishes the human. But the comedic effect is no less decisive if the human participant appears to keep up in good order with the system: the desire to become part of the machine or system hysterizes the shared interaction, marking both system and participants as united in their absurd over-efficiency. This is what Bergson means by our capacity to find humour in conscious and unconscious automatism: the feeling that in watching the maintenance of a repetitive and inelastic act, efficiency serves only to heighten a futile obstinacy. Laughter then in this instance has a capacity to correct the perceived imbalance between human capacity and system, insofar as the submission of humans to the logic of indifferent rationalization shows how much of this kind of rationalization is the enemy of life and vitality. So, for Bergson, under industrial modernity what falls to the comedic and humorous is a specific social role: the exposure of the increasing unbending abstraction of productive and social life as an encroachment into human contingency and finitude. Hence, the importance of the fact that during early modernism the comedic is placed directly in the line of fire against the human-technology duality: i.e. the comedic disruption of unthinking efficiency serves, at its most insistent and radical, to reveal how the industrialization and militarization of technology prepares workers and citizens ultimately for conflict and violence, and as such for the erosion of

[5] Henri Bergson, *Laughter: An Essay on the Meaning of the Comic*, Green Integer, Copenhagen and Los Angeles, 1999

human relationality and generosity. Picabia, Kafka and Fallada all fall into this comedic spirit of exposing enforced, empty constraint, in which the human is made to appear as a kind of ridiculous extraneous input into material forces beyond humans' direct control. (We see this also in Charlie Chaplin's film *Modern Times* [1936] in which the speed of the production line turns Chaplin less into an efficient and muscular worker than a sexual predator in which, overstimulated by the repetitive labour of the production line, women for Chaplin become objects to be technically adjusted with spanners, encouraging him further, in the next scene – undiminished in his excessive energy – into a hyperactive lever-pusher and knob-twiddler, oblivious to what he's doing.) Indeed, for Kafka, egress from the objectifying conditions of this kind of human extraneousness is utterly opaque, in the end a matter of arbitrary judgement, which makes the humour of his hero K's relationship with the self-justifying and slippery edicts and instructions of the encounter with state power and its technicalities in *The Trial* all the more funny. In fact, the unrelenting evasion of power's responsibility, its absolute unwillingness to be transparent on its own terms, strangely makes its terror appear fictive and thus vacuous, stupid and vulnerable; what announces itself as the Big Other in the novel, ends as a dismal, inflated Potemkin-like structure.

But for other early modernist artists the human-technology duality is not just evidence of technology as social catastrophe and the need for art and humanity to find an exit from technology as an exit from human extraneousness. Earlier I mentioned Duchamp's unassisted readymades. Duchamp's readymades catapult the artist not into the misery of human extraneousness but into a rational engagement with technology and labour power. In *Fountain,* the presentation of a shop-bought factory made urinal translates the deskilling of craft in the production process into a general reflection on art's place in the modern division of labour and as such a recognition of art's subjection to new technical requirements after the erosion of art's traditional artisanal base. Duchamp's unassisted readymades are not anti-art *gestes,* but material claims on a new technical relation in art, and therefore establish a new working relationship between artistic skill, technology, and conceptualization. The artist is no longer merely the aesthetic arbitrator of the human-technology duality, but the technical investigator of technology's productive and social domains and capacities. The artist *thinks* technology as a condition of using, reusing, and misusing it. The artist inserts himself or herself into the technical demands of technology-as-system, transforming the terms and conditions of artistic skill, diminishing art's aesthetic privileges – as a condition of art's would-be freedoms – from the machino-technical extension of the human. The artist is now first and foremost a producer, and, as such, is no less integrated into the technological instrumentalities of industrial capitalism, as are the factory worker and office worker.

This move towards the artist as producer and technician was formalized, of course, under the innovative interdisciplinary demands of the avant-garde during the Russian Revolution, when constructivism opened up a systematic encounter between technology, technique and social transformation. Here all residual attachments to art as aesthetic contemplation were destroyed as the artist's relationship to technology was for the first time derived from the intersection of art's environmental and social extension. Artists began to build things that contribute to the refunctioning of the physical world and social relations, looking beyond the production of discrete objects to design and architecture for their social-relational bearings. Indeed, Romantic anti-technologism, and the miseries of human extraneousness, were swept away in the anticipated incorporation of artistic technique into general social technique (technical systems) as outlined in Boris Arvatov's *Art and Production* (*Iskusstvo i proizvodstvo*) published in Moscow in 1926, which above all stresses art's social use-values and egalitarian levelling under the new machino-technical culture.[6] Art

---

[6] Boris Arvatov, *Art and Production*, eds. John Roberts and Alexei Penzin, Pluto Press, London, 2017

and technology combine as a common product of worker, technician and artist (as technician).

In this respect this incorporation of artistic technique into general social technique has determined the template for constructivist approaches to art and technology in the 20th century down to the new post-digital promethean 'constructivisms' of today. [7] Technology and *technē* are seen as integral to definitions of the human, and its cognitive and biophysical extension; there is no humanness without technical extension and human interaction with, and learning from, machines and the realities of art's extended place in the division of labour. But the constructivist experiments of the Soviet avant-garde were short lived; what remained of their revolutionary and utopic spirit after the Stalinist Thermidor was brutally subordinated to state-patriotism and the instrumentalization of Soviet 'life-building', removing from the development of technology all creative feedback processes that might enhance the quality of life. The increasing Soviet industrial and military competition with Europe and the USA rendered the creative misuse of technology not just superfluous but wasteful. Technology's principal virtue was the undergirding of defence, state security and economic growth.

As such, under Cold War conditions after 1945, there was a radical collapse of a non-deterministic and social model of art and technology more broadly, despite the drive on the part of the USA and its allies, after the destruction of Europe and South East Asia and large parts of the Soviet Union, to rebuild the collapse of global superstructures on principles of public accountability and the state funding of science and technology, and the mobilization of the public will and civic responsibility. For even though some people were willing to accept government talk about peacetime

---

[7] See for example *Speculative Aesthetics*, eds. Robin Mackay, James Trafford, and Luke Pendrell, Urbanomic, Falmouth, 2014; *Construction Site for Possible Worlds*, eds. Amanda Beech, Robin Mackay, and James Wiltgen, Urbanomic, Falmouth, 2020

technological progress, there was growing resistance to the new Cold War militarization; governments might spin technological progress to some effect, but for the generation who fought and suffered there was no simple assimilation of the trauma of the war years into postwar democracy; science and technology, consequently, were unable to fully escape the imaginaries of social regression, so incisively mapped out in Theodor Adorno and Max Horkheimer's *Dialectic of Enlightenment* in 1944,[8] and were pulled back tightly by popular opinion in the 1950s into the technological catastrophism of the 1920s and 1930s. There was little trust in science and technology-for-peace, dominated as postwar talk of progress was by the destructive aftermaths of the Holocaust, Hiroshima and Nagasaki, and the continuing militarization of the world's biggest economies (USA, Britain, France, and the Soviet Union). The postwar democratic glow soon dissipated. It was clear the victory of the allies under the hegemony of the USA required a less sanguine narrative: the war's destruction of a pre-war authoritarianism and conservatism across Europe was not simply a clearing away of those forces that prevented 'democratic modernization', but in reality a path for American capital to rapidly modernize those market capitalist forces already in place in its own interests, as a means of securing a privileged economic place for the USA in the détente between east and west, and a new regime of accumulation. After the global violence of the war the global violence of new technology in Europe and North America – of mass consumption and mass communication – appears to grow without reserve, bringing humanity under even greater subordination to rational administration and scientific bureaucracy and the discipline of technical efficiency; the necessary costs, as governments would say, of Western progress. These feelings of constraint and mass submission, underscored by the unassimilated trauma of the war years, produced a familiar kind of aestheticized distanciation on the part of artists from technology and science. The idea that the artist might establish a

---

[8] Theodor Adorno and Max Horkheimer, *Dialectic of Enlightenment*, Verso, London and New York, 2016

technical investment in changing the agendas of technology appeared risible; the only realistic move was to step back and find some aesthetic correlative, some chastened space separate from the instrumental uses of technology. Indeed, the postwar radical collapse of the utopic constructivist imaginary and return to images of catastrophism is no better illustrated by the widespread shift in art in the late 1940s, 1950s and early 1960s to the violent and distressed presentation of technologies and machines and machine parts as archaic and ugly remnants from a ruined world, in which the artist is again the aesthetic beholder of disaster and hubris and keeper of the flame of anti-technological humanness, but harnessed to a vision that is far darker than Picabia's playful re-articulation of machine parts. In this instance machine parts are fused with body parts in charred mortification, as in Eduardo Paolozzi's bronzes; or crushed into inchoateness as in John Chamberlain's automobile sculptures; or accumulated as violent crash-site images in Wolf Vostell's graphic techno-industrial photo archives. The artist, now, invariably believed that there was no living place for art inside the human-technology duality, beyond that is, the artist giving himself or herself up wholly cynically to the role of state employee and cheerleader for technological progress in the democratic age of automobiles and rockets; the artist experienced only shame in front of technological rationalism, and therefore felt no commitment to reimagining technology's hoped-for beneficent creative powers.

Yet the spirit of technological constructivism doesn't entirely disappear from art and literature in the postwar period; a few artists and writers resist the lures of human extraneousness in order to call up a version of the (Duchampian) artist-as-technician that holds to some non-catastrophic account of technological use values, and to a critique of technology that places humans and the technosystem into some creative relation. There is some evidence of this in the group Fluxus, in artists trying to build actions and systems that reclaim the idea of making as a non-dominative encounter with things and people. John Cage, Takako Saito, Mieko

Shiomi, Shigeko Kubota, and later Nam June Paik fit in here.[9] But I am struck by how one writer in particular, during this period, in an intriguingly heterogeneous body of work, resists the catastrophism of the war in order to bring into working relationship the technological system and the concrete language of misuse and creative adaptation, which is directly pertinent to our arguments here in relation to Micheál O'Connell's own ad hoc version of constructivism and to the overall shape and dynamic of what a non-deterministic critique of technology in art might look like today. This is Flann O'Brien. This choice might seem an equally strange and easy comparison: strange, given, that O'Brien is not noted for his formal contribution to the debate on art and technology, and easy, given O'Brien and O'Connell's shared comedic deflationary strategies and invocation of the lingering myths and doxa of ancient and modern 'Irishness' that can provide some kind of comfortable historical continuity and therefore give sustenance to the idea that our reading of O'Connell's art would work best if it is mediated by Irish history and Irish artistic precedents. Firstly, there is nothing specifically Irish about O'Connell's critique of technology, or the cognitive and technical concerns of the work, but there is a recognizable link between his comedic entry point into art and the history of technology and colonialism and the Irish experience. One might say that giving up the temptations of paddywhackery in his comedy routine was precisely evidence of this: he recognized how easy it is to internalize the colonial relation in order to 'get a laugh' from UK audiences. But in self-consciously releasing himself from this relation, resisting the *jouissance* to please through subversion ('look, I'm not a threat, but the things I say have a sting in the tail, and will enliven you, titillate you') he realizes that the colonial

---

[9] One of the first writers to deal with the post-Duchampian relationship between art, technology, and systems interference (cybernetics) was Jack Burnham, albeit from a position of fetishized modernity and blithe 'up-to-dateness'. See *Beyond Modern Sculpture: The Effects of Science and Technology on the Sculpture of This Century*, George Braziller, New York, 1968

relation is still whirring away, still pressing home its advantage. That is, no matter how he reconstructs his artistic identity as a Britain-domiciled cosmopolitan and post-national radical, his place in the technosystem, his own libidinal attachment to seeing it splutter and falter and make a fool of itself, is subjectively disclosed by thinking technology from an anti-colonial perspective. O'Connell may be a 'post-art technician', a computer literate vector of the life of algorithms, and deflator of the emoting humanist artist, but he inhabits the technosystem from a specific cultural and historical perspective, a perspective that is overdetermined by the subjectivity of the colonial relation, of emigration, of the lingering afterlife of British condescension and power. In the work for the show at Uillinn: West Cork Arts Centre, made mostly in Ireland, or thought about in Ireland, the idea of speaking to technology, through technology, is configured, sometimes directly, sometimes obliquely, through the history of technology in Ireland and Ireland's place today in the global economy and transnational networks of platform capitalism. In other words, thrumming away in the background of his show is the radically uneven position of Irish capitalism as an economic periphery, from its days of agrarian somnolence and small-scale industries at the beginning of the 20th century, to the leaping Celtic Tiger of the 1990s, with its tax breaks for international capital, housing boom, and the rapid growth in new biotech and digital industries, all undercut by the long and tendentious struggle nationally throughout this historical sequence about how modern a modern Ireland should be. A lot, a little, ah, go on then, less than a lot and more than a little.[10] And this is what makes the connection with O'Brien compelling for our discussion here, for more than any other modern Irish writer he directly involved himself in these discussions about modernity and modernization in a period in Ireland whose context, uniquely, afforded a non-catastrophist and social-relational approach to technology, as a condition of thinking

---

[10] For a discussion of the Irish boom and post-2008 crisis, see Seán Ó Riain, *The Rise and Fall of Ireland's Celtic Tiger: Liberalism, Boom and Bust*, Cambridge University Press, Cambridge, 2014

the modern from the perspective – as in other global peripheries – of those who have little control over what the modern might be. In other words, I believe we can pick up some anti-colonialist insights from O'Brien's varied interventions into the human-technology relation so as we can clarify some wider issues around the artistic 'constructivism' of O'Connell's 'system interference'. If we can also show how this is mediated by a deflationary, comedic, anti-colonialist Irish perspective, so much the better.

Flann O'Brien, the novelist (birth name Brian O'Nolan), worked as a journalist under the pseudonym of Myles na Gopaleen for the *Irish Times* from 1940 through the 1950s, contributing a satirical column *Cruiskeen Lawn* most days during this period. In 1939 he published *At Swim-Two-Birds,* a novel charting the drinking and phantasmatical storytelling of a poor Dublin student (a novel much admired by James Joyce) and in 1941 a pastiche of Oirishy mud-and-potato goings-on in deepest farming country novel written in Irish, *An Béal Bocht* (*Poor Mouth*). As he was to say in a letter to Seán O'Casey in 1942: "It is an honest attempt to get under the skin of a certain type of 'Gael', which I find the most nauseating phenomenon in Europe."[11] The novel he's most well-known for, *The Third Policeman,* was finished soon after *At Swim-Two-Birds,* but rejected by publishers in the 1950s and published in 1967 a year after his death. His active writing career, therefore, consisted mostly of his satirical columns, which remarkably were allowed a huge amount of free-wheeling autonomy and were extremely popular. Few people knew Myles na Gopaleen was Flann O'Brien and even fewer knew na Gopaleen was Brian O'Nolan, a leading civil servant, who became private secretary to two ministers for local government (civil servants were not allowed to publish under their own names). Indeed, na Gopaleen's column is remarkable for its blending of fictive provocation and the development of a kind of civil service imagination, in which the public persona of na

---

[11] 'Letter to Seán Casey', *The Collected Letters of Flann O'Brien,* ed. Maebh Long, Dalkey Archive Press, Dallas, London, and Dublin, 2018, p116

Gopaleen, as a 'man of knowledge', his relentless attentiveness to national social problems and the amelioration of niggling inconveniences, restrictive social niceties, poorly conceived public works and under-attained and delivered public services, becomes the basis for the na Gopaleen Research Bureau. O'Brien, then, constructs a vivid proxy voice in which his role of public busybody in the columns veils a genuine interest and satisfaction on O'Brien's part in the artistic and technical refunctioning of machinic and technological systems. In his identity as 'chief researcher and inventor' for the Research Bureau (grounded, in actuality, in his rigorous administrative skills as a civil servant) he brings various kinds of creative misuse to the rethinking of technologies and machines, or the creation of new technologies, in the Republic. As such he is constantly chivvying institutions, local government, the good and the great, manufacturers, to think of ways in which the lives of Dubliners and the Irish might meet the new demands of modernity and the new Ireland, by adopting the Research Bureau's innovative services or convenience-devices. [12] The Bureau is a veritable banker for new ideas, na Gopaleen insists. It receives nearly a thousand letters a day from readers he boasts, "asking us to devise machines and engines that will serve their personal problems".[13] But these services and devices, for all their earnest presentation, are invariably technologies, machines or services or surveys that are fanciful, arbitrary, inconsequential, decorative, adventitious, indeed, that mostly encourage indolence or support various kinds of affectation. A few examples will give us a sense

---

[12] A version of the public busybody, as a publicly minded nuisance, was taken up at the beginning of Thatcherism by the satirical writer William Donaldson under the pseudonym of Henry Root, who took it upon himself to write to the 'good and the great' about multiple minor inconveniencies, falling public standards, and British national failings. See *The Henry Root Letters*, Sphere, London, 1981

[13] Myles na Gopaleen, 'Uproot the Youth Rot!', *The Best of Myles*, Picador, London, 1977, p121

where the priorities of the Research Bureau lie in O'Brien's search for Irish technological advantage and progress:

A mechanical 'book handler' which 'reads' your books for you, slightly discolouring them, and bending the pages, so as to show friends and guests that your library is well read. In fact, he goes one better: there is no need to choose any books in the first place, the Myles na Gopaleen Book Club will select books for you *already rubbed*, "You are spared the trouble of soiling and mauling"[14] any purchased book yourself.

A device for overweight ballet dancers, worried that they are too out of shape and can longer "leap the requisite six feet", which na Gopaleen calls the 'Myles' Patent Ballet Pumps, and which allows the dancers' shoes to be "fitted with three diminutive land mines, one in the heel and one in each side of the front foot", enabling on explosion, to send the dancer "flying through the air with the greatest of ease".[15]

The creation of a Writers, Actors, Artists, Musicians Association (WAAMA), an escort agency for cultural events in which hired persons do the hard work of applause, cultural chit-chat and approbation for you.

A household snow-melting machine made of copper and consisting "of a funnel or catch-pipe for the snow, which widens inwardly, then drops eighteen inches, allowing the snow to fall into a pan beneath", to be melted by hot water in a surrounding pan, the water then running into a gauged bucket, enabling the owner when visited by a melancholic artist or aesthete, fop or young lover on snowy days, who asks longingly, "Mais où sont les neiges

---

[14] Myles na Gopaleen, 'Book Handling', ibid, p22
[15] Myles na Gopaleen, 'Sufferers Helped', ibid, pp26–28

d'antan?" ("Where are the snows of yesteryear?"), to point effortlessly at the bucket.[16]

A stopwatch that acts as a thermometer, which worn inside your clothes takes your temperature all day – the patent valetudinarian's vadamecum.

The efficient lighting of street lamps from sewer gas, through the introduction of a mechanism into the street lamp that "refines, vaporises and ignites the sewer gas, which is then transmitted to incandescent mantles in the globe higher up".

A new kind of ink, "trink", that when applied to paper and dried, produces an alcoholic vapour, "which will hang over the document in an invisible and odourless cloud for several days...Intoxication ensues, mild or acute, according to how much reading is done", allowing eventually for the possibility that national newspapers will adapt the idea, so as to give each reader a "lightning pick-me-up".[17]

A substitute for a much coveted "midnight oil", a patent midnight grease derived from turf, whiskey, offal and cider, which burns with a "pale blue flame".[18]

Patent emergency trousers for the Plain People of Ireland that are fitted with "long eel-like pockets"[19] that can facilitate the storing of four bottles of stout in each leg.

A new kind of mixer tap that allows the user to draw hot water or cold water or both simultaneously to a preferred temperature.

---

[16] Myles na Gopaleen, 'A Handy Instrument', ibid, pp112–113
[17] Myles na Gopaleen 'Our Aim', ibid, p118
[18] Myles na Gopaleen, 'Uproot the Youth Rot!', ibid, p124
[19] Myles na Gopaleen, 'Research Bureau', ibid, p126

A telephone that calls at a prearranged times to generate a maximum status effect for the owner in front of friends or family ('hello Taoiseach, good to hear from you').

A patent spring-top hat that on contact pops up to protect the owner from falling debris.

These are all artfully conceived devices and services which turn for comic effect on the pinpointing and gameful solution of various public health, energy and social issues, and questions of social etiquette, and which appear to be inconsequential to say the least. Great technical and administrative ingenuity is devoted to the solution of minor, abstruse or implausible problems and inconveniences. Or so it would seem. Firstly, the concern given over to superfluity hides a practical inventiveness that demonstrates in some instances good design sense and the meeting creatively of unmet needs: who doesn't have access to hot/cold mixer taps these days; and those large pockets in your cargo pants are perfect for quick visits to the off-licence; and haven't I seen that watch-body thermometer as an app somewhere? But secondly, and more crucially, the technical creativity, born of a spirit of getting by and making do, openly defies and mocks the higher and sublime reaches of technology, to find – indeed, engineer – a very different relationship to technology than that associated with the war years and the techno-catastrophism of the previous decades: a relationship to *technē* and technology that, through its humour and inconsequentiality, actually gives visible form to people's unthought and barely imagined needs. Who doesn't want an ice melter attached to the roof of their house for those awkward moments on very cold days with friends, when cruel memories of lost snows are just too painful for your friends to contemplate? In this sense na Gopaleen provides an interesting point of creative subalternity in response to the human-technology duality in this period of violent state-technophilia (many of the inventions above were conceived during the war years [or 'The Emergency' as it was officially called] with its shortages and rationing, and its austere aftermath). The inventions, driven by a crafty misuse of materials and indifference to conventional forms of functionality, subvert the dominant war economy and the technological catastrophism that accompanies it to inhabit a world of technological relations and objects in which technical ingenuity can ameliorate certain miseries or challenge social rigidities or conformities by bringing a multitude of localized and individuated solutions – self-delighting solutions – to bear on the frustrating particulars and conventions of everyday life. In this respect, the humorous indifference to functionality, or more pertinently the radical sense of other non-instrumental kinds of functionality, has an eager Dada spirit to them. And certainly, O'Brien had some familiarity with this period of the avant-garde, and saw himself as the (Irish) literary heir to its moment of anti-bourgeois negation and dyspeptic distaste for the metaphysics of efficiency. He was a scholar of interwar European modernism and its complex unravelling of sense experience.[20] Perhaps the best way of describing O'Brien's writing is as Irish science fiction, but without rockets and space travel and interstellar warfare; an Irish science fiction that doesn't physically leave Earth's atmosphere, and that is happy to plod along country roads and Dublin's back streets. But in addition, and perhaps more crucially, there is also a shared spirit here with the three female postwar Japanese artists I mention above: Takako Saito, Mieko Shiomi, Shigeko Kubota. This is an extraordinary generation of Japanese artists and musicians, particularly women artists, some who moved to New York in the 1950s and later hooked up with Fluxus, and some who stayed in Japan, who, in order to work through and reinhabit the human-technology duality after atomic

---

[20] For a wide-ranging reflection on Paris, Duchamp and the interwar post-Dada dynamic of this destabilization of the vernacular (of design grammars and rules of drawing) of popular science (of diagrammatic knowledge, correct mensuration and pedagogic exercises), see Molly Nesbit, *Their Common Sense*, Black Dog Publishing, London, 2000. O'Brien's humorous, refunctioning of capitalism's techno-scientific world, and inversion or qualification of efficiency, derives from this mostly 1920s and 1930s Duchampian project.

destruction, defied the subjection of the Japanese people to the animality of the victor's colonial vision, and its imperialist and racist justification of the obliteration of Japanese citizens at Hiroshima and Nagasaki as a necessity of war, by living out the human-technology duality as place of quiet and pacific attention to the nourishing contingencies of technologies and systems. Rather than submitting to the imperialist histories of technology and to the relentless logic of violence and interstate warfare, and as such to a Japanese version of aesthetic distanciation, or invoking the symbols of 'people's tragedy' as the cost of postwar defeat – the Allied version of reconciliation – this generation of Japanese artists remove the evidence of technological violence, of burnt and eviscerated bodies, as a condition of resisting historical necessity and the ideology of victimhood immediately imposed on the Japanese people at the end of the war. Subverting both Japanese fascism and American imperialism alike, these artists sought new rationalities, new attachments, from the creation of open and stochastic systems of materials, actions, relations, and sounds, in which technology, *technē* and human intervention form indeterminate outcomes and patterns of meaning. Technology as the delivery of systems that deliver death is neither the actuality of systems nor of technology. Systems are human-determined even if the systems are themselves based on extra-human calculations and computation. Thus, in the late 1950s and early 1960s these young Japanese women artists sought a space for art's place in the artistic deposition of absolute necessity, through the creation of new and low-scale systems of post-medium-specific production that insisted on the non-instrumental potentialities of technology (Kubuto's early video work) and on the invited unanticipated points of interaction and spontaneous at-a-distance-collaboration globally between artists and non-artists, such as Shiomi's 'spatial poems'. Sending out by mail various simple instructions to selected recipients as a guide to action, the invited participants to her events are only notionally defined by the requirements of the requests, producing overall a highly porous and aleatory expansion of the original instructions. As was to become common in the 1960s, the anti-systematization of systems and the systemization of antisystematicity determined the calculable and non-calculable boundaries of spontaneity and improvisation in art, producing performance works and forms of music that pursued and favoured how the reproduction of systems not governed by narrowly preset options and pathways of action can release unexpected fluctuations, divergences, excesses, and hidden micro-relations, that constantly transform iterations of the given system. Thus, the priority given to feedback loops in 'system interference' becomes identifiable with the recalibration of the boundaries of the system itself; the system is what is made from the changing elements and potentialities of the relations involved, allowing the systems to become open and future-oriented. One can therefore see what a flipped history of art and technology under these war conditions and imperialism would look like from the position of these women artists and their critique of a victim-centred and exclusionary account of technology: women no longer appear pinioned inside male machinic fantasies of control, or the domesticated adjuncts of technology efficiency in office and home, or the extruded, brutalized remnants of war machines, but as agents defined by their technical and rational relationship to events and materials. In this sense this is an extraordinarily important moment for women artists, prior to first wave feminism. This is the point where women artists define themselves for the first time by their technical adroitness.

O'Brien shares something of this open and future oriented approach to systems. His decolonializing misuse of technology opens up a critical space between non-aligned, neutral and 'little' nations, against the destructive, controlling technologies of the imperialist war machine. Indeed, one of the strange overlaps between his *Cruiskeen Lawn* column and the young postwar Japanese modernists, is that na Gopaleen excludes any reference to the war and its military technologies, as if Ireland's exclusion from the violence of the second world war as a neutral nation required an exclusion of Ireland from any representational taint with the dominant technological imaginary of imperialism. Progress, here, obliquely, is figured through some special, localized, non-colonizing relationship to technique and technology, a flourishing of native wit and ingenuity in the face of rationing and shortages, rather than the projection of big-screen fantasies about instrumental reason and the New Ireland. This is why the modernizing antibureaucratic character of O'Brien's inventions have a peculiar *retardataire* feeling, despite their striking and hopeful confrontation with the bureaucratic inertia of postwar Irish society. That is, the prevailing voice of O'Brien's 'system interference' – for purposes of humour and acceptability – is the conservative and sardonic inventor at war with bureaucratic inefficiency. His understanding of system interference is far closer to the dominant sexualized terrain of male anti-bureaucratism of interwar modernism, in which the male inventor or visionary takes on the irrationality of a bureaucratic system in the name of 'the people', 'national rejuvenation' or 'progress', as a means of highlighting its failure of claims to efficiency. His misuse of technology and technical knowledge in these terms, then, fulfils the conventional role of popular-democratic scientific-inventor investigator, even if it is shaped by Dadaistic and transgressive imperatives, and, as such, is subject in comedic vein to all the familiar self-inflating notions of the egoistic and combative male artist, confronted with what his inventor idiot-savant de Selby calls in *The Third Policeman* the "pedestrian intellects of the unperceiving laity",[21] i.e. everybody else. Hence O'Brien's comedic 'man of knowledge' is perhaps far closer to Charlie Chaplin's unregulated egoists than to John Cage's discreet, collaborative, and queer subversion of system, given his overidentification with decolonialization as a kind of modernist sandblasting of effete and demasculinized bureaucratic thinking. Indeed, there is little place for women in his decolonializing vision of demotic technique, technology, and pleasure, insofar as women are held to exist largely outside of the techno-scientific relation, things to be talked past or pitied when it comes to technical understanding. Which is why women seem such a weak or absent presence in O'Brien's

---

[21] Flann O'Brien, *The Third Policeman*, Harper Perennial Modern Classics, HarperCollins, London and New York, 2007, p152

novels themselves; there is barely one convincing female character in *At Swim-Two-Birds* and *The Third Policeman*, or one compelling line addressed to a woman, despite the fact that these two novels are preoccupied with male neurosis and destructive obsessional behaviour, confined as his leading male characters tend to be to their own misapprehensions and impotencies, as in the case of de Selby. "Another of de Selby's weaknesses was his inability to distinguish between men and women."[22] Mysteriously he called his mother "a very distinguished gentleman".[23]

---

[22] Flann O'Brien, ibid, p173
[23] Flann O'Brien, ibid, p174

## Chapter 2: Abduction and Stupidity

So, having taken this detour, where might we place O'Connell's own 'system interference', when questions of heteroclite invention and the creation of an ironized 'man of knowledge' or simple defences of system openness, seem like reduced imaginative options for the artist today confronted with a technosystem whose power and extension are now vast and ubiquitous, and as such have completed the technical incorporation of the artist into the art-technology relation? Indeed, the two figures I discuss here, the open-system anti-systematizer and the quirky inventor, have been incorporated deep into the computational logic of the contemporary technosystem, as the programmed irruptive agents behind the future and creative life of algorithms. Nevertheless, these two figures, are certainly not *locked in* there inside the technosystem's version of creativity; both still have a strong and determining relationship with humour – and humour, if anything, defies computation to keep a straight face and follow a straight line to probability. In O'Connell's work we still see the comedic and sardonic as an escape route from the self-rationalizing logic of technological systems, systems that know only the limited preset human terms of their rationality and interface with the world. On this score, we might say that O'Connell passes through the figures of the anti-systematizers and comedic, inventor-technicians in order to produce an idea of the artist who doesn't want to either build new machines or make the anti-systematic and open potentialities of machines more like ordinary creative humans. As he says, which I will discuss later: he has no interest in adding any new objects to the world, certainly any that are defined by their technical *artisticness*. He talks of having a discomfort with making in these terms. Rather, he wants, in the devolved spirit of O'Brien and Dada, and the voice of the feminized male ingénue, and Japanese Fluxus, to play stupid with technology, through the creative and exemplary misuse of their outcomes and internal logics. I say *play* stupid, then, because *being* stupid is no help to anyone, let alone artists, as Avital Ronell explains in her wide-ranging enfilading of the word's multiple meanings and misunderstandings in *Stupidity* (2003).[24] No artist of any ambition actually wants to be stupid, because being stupid means you've already excluded yourself from being an artist and from critical thought. There are no good or interesting stupid artists who arrive as if by chance, as of the Gods; there is only 'thinking stupid' artists, who give all their thought to stupidity in order to avoid the encroachment of stupidity, like Paul McCarthy in his portrayal of the artist-as-child-as-psychotic in his video *Painter* (1995), an emoting, self-harming, hammy, self-pitying, expressionist painter, who eventually chops off his fingers and chants "de Kooning, de Kooning de Kooning", as if unconsciously trying to ward off the pain of his demonstrable and deathly stupidity. In this sense, envoicing stupidity is a bit like Jacques Derrida's pharmakon: the poison that provides the antidote – that is, an oxymoronic intervention that takes the presentation of the problem to be part of the cure. As Ronell says: "For its part, stupidity can body-snatch intelligence, disguise itself…"[25] as does McCarthy in his video. So stupid must do what stupid must do as thinking idiocy, as the body-snatching work that exposes stupidity and announces non-stupidity, in order – in the light of our concerns here – for the artist to fully harness comedy's disruptive capture of the limits of technological rationality, and thereby expose the deeply absurd and craven link between calculability, progress, and capitalist reason.

In his PhD thesis, *Art as 'Artificial Stupidity'* (2016),[26] and published and unpublished papers over the past 12 years, O'Connell has been increasingly sensitized to what I called earlier Bergson's chief psychological insight into modern industrial life: that laughter is

---

[24] Avital Ronell, *Stupidity*, University of Illinois Press, Urbana and Chicago, 2003
[25] Avital Ronell, ibid, p10
[26] Micheál O'Connell, *Art as 'Artificial Stupidity'*, PhD thesis, University of Sussex, 2016

well-placed to reveal or release the inflated expenditure of technologies and their claims to efficiency. That this humour can fall away into aestheticized gentility, or tedious observations that machines break down, is obvious, but it can also lay claim to a more capacious sense of 'thinking stupidity' that questions the very capitalist 'natural rights' of machine intelligence. In this sense O'Connell's 'system interference' is less concerned with pointing out the local inefficiencies in our use of technologies under digital platform capitalism, than establishing, in a more metaphysically charged sense, the general obtuseness and stupefyingness of the technosystem as a whole, despite the technology's claims for speed and preparedness. And in this sense, what concerns him, precisely contrary to this self-image of digitalized free market transparency, is that the 'life of algorithms', far from being the work of computer-enhanced creativity is, rather, the outcome of the uniform and calculated actions of a hidden and high-speed bureaucracy: the bureaucracy of the market. The creative life of algorithms is no more nor less the lining up consumers with the statistical processing and management of preselected desires. Indeed, O'Connell talks about the unacknowledged social cost of the present digital technosystem as a kind of a bureaucratic *rationing*. "If apps and platforms are somehow equivalent to bureaucracy, then contrary to their appearance as facilitators of access to goods, services and knowledge, their actual effect could be more akin to rationing."[27]

The deepening shift to a computational-based technological 'control society' since the early 1990s can be seen loosely, therefore, as operable through the intersection of users and consumers with 'scripts' (rules of conduct, axioms, principles of action, modes of attention, directives, lists, diagrams, tables, maps, formulae, instructions) which do not simply take on the appearance of social reality for the user, but facilitate the notion that the subject's access to services and goods is actually co-extensive with their self-

---

[27] Micheál O'Connell, '(Bad) Faith in the Algorithm: Bureaucracy, Democracy and Tricksterism', unpublished paper, 2021, p8

determining access to this reality itself. But if these digital forms of attention and provision form an entelechial structure, rarely are these control 'scripts' strictly commands, unless the law and the state are directly involved. Rather, as points of freely accessed market facilitation (which increasingly cover social goods, such as health and education, as well as banking and shopping) they are always being tailored to algorithmic evidence of the subject's changing needs or circumstances and choice, weakening any sense of the calculability and the 'scriptedness' of the interaction between user, machine, and information. Digital technology doesn't command – it provides a kind of *inertial open structure* that cleverly closes out non-market exit points ('stay with us, it is the only rational thing to do'), prompting at all points for the user that they need to think constructively about their time and resources and what the multiplicitousness of digital platforms generously offer. For, non-electronically mediated alternative points of access to information, services, goods, and other lives, can only lead ultimately to non-connectedness and thus to the creation of inefficient and de-socialized citizens, and a drop in libidinal attachment to the digital life. Indeed, one of the most successful and algorithmic 'scripts' or building blocks of the internet and social media that drives this entelechy of technological connectedness is the use of homophily by tech providers: that is, the application of the law of association, of the same, as a means of capturing the pleasures of familiarity and lessening the threat of cognitive dissonance and anxiety linked with the threat of the unknown. In these terms homophily is the affective and ideological glue that underlies the digital 'script' as both facilitator of choice and the pleasures of familiarity, of knowing what one wants based on what one already wants and knows: in other words, it creates comforting and fixed boundaries predicated on the perceived democratic creation of shared interests or 'likes', and therefore encourages the production of shared patterns of efficient and predictable communication and mutual support. As such, homophily's primary function under these conditions is the creation of self-protecting clusters of the 'like-minded', erasing conflict and disagreement at the same time as protecting difference.

Indeed, homophily is the very epistemological ground of network science and Big Data', subtly exercising the ideal of shared difference as the creative rationale of market democracy. Association and pattern recognition always trump causation and history. But, as a consequence, this homophilic protection of difference leads inevitably to the assumption that sociality is no more than a constellation of multiple aggregations, intersecting at some points, but largely indifferent or unaware of the relationship between different aggregate clusters and the social whole and of those divisions and unities that bisect them. As Wendy Hui Kyong Chun argues, this model of networked self-protection fundamentally weakens the concept of society at the same time as it nominally extends the formal content of electronic socialization globally. "Neoliberalism destroys society by proliferating neighborhoods. Networks preempt and predict by reading all singular actions as indications of larger collective habitual patterns, based not on our individual actions but rather the actions of others. Correlations, that is, are not made based solely on an individual's actions and history but rather the history and actions of others 'like' him or her."[28] Thus, under these conditions the human-technology interface and the question of 'system interference' takes on a very different logic. The call for open-ended systems and non-instrumental uses of technology will as a priority need to be fundamentally attached to the analysis and knowledge of what network algorithms do and fail to as the basis for transcending homophily and its fetishization of connectedness under market democracy. There is then a critical and practical priority attached to this reality: the need for the rewriting or recoding of the homophilic algorithm as the basis of any radical refunctioning of digital culture. There needs to be, as Chun says, a technical queering of homophily as a denaturalization of the logic of markets and the breaking of its dominant code of 'connectedness', as

---

[28] Wendy Hui Kyong Chun, 'Queerying Homophily', in Clemens Apprich, Wendy Hui Kyong Chun, Florian Cramer and Hito Steyerl, *Pattern Discrimination*, meson press, Lüneberg, and University of Minnesota Press, Minneapolis, 2018, p75

opposed simply to the production of detached, aestheticized forms of artistic or critical negation. O'Connell, in a notional sense agrees with this, as I have stressed. His model of 'system interference' relies on this technical commitment to change on the part of the artist, and concomitantly, the technical knowledges this requires. As such, this draws on what we might call an expressly political third model of 'system interference' – in addition to open-ended system refunctioning and creative *technē* – that is identifiable with our current digital age: namely, the move from an aestheticized or DIY alternative-technology encounter with the modern technosystem to the *critical* immersion of practice into the technological life. The best exposition of this position is one of the earliest in fact, and one that is strikingly close to Chun and her fellow critics of homophily: the Critical Art Ensemble's anti-aesthetic, hacker and tech-artist 'manifesto', *The Electronic Disturbance,* published in 1994.[29] In important respects the group lays out some of the key requirements of a 'system interference' model of artistic practice that would be equal to the radical challenges of the new network technosystem emerging in the early 1990s: a rejection of "aestheticized retreatism" in favour of technical know-how and creativity;[30] the production of a mode of 'system interference' that disturbs or liquidates the structures of "habitual passive consumption";[31] a rejection of the photographic or video image as the primary and overdetermined cognitive focus for artistic content (always a temptation for the aesthetic position); an analytic emphasis on the oppressive temporalities of techno-culture as source of emancipatory reflection on technology as such; the creation of practices and modes of action that increase the artist's "degree of autonomy in electronic space"; [32] and the production, even, of an "aesthetics *of* inefficiency", opposed, that is, to an *aesthetics* of inefficiency: "The aesthetic of inefficiency, of

---

[29] Critical Art Ensemble, *The Electronic Disturbance,* Autonomedia, Brooklyn, New York, 1994
[30] Critical Art Ensemble, ibid, p20
[31] Critical Art Ensemble, ibid, p52
[32] Critical Art Ensemble, ibid, p124

desperate gambles, of incommensurable imaginings, of insufferable interruptions, are all part of individual sovereignty. These are situations in which invention occurs."[33]

O'Connell's version of 'system interference' takes this de-aestheticized and technical path from the Critical Art Ensemble to Chun. But the role of the artist as interlocuter cannot be fixed by this technical role alone, and therefore the notion that it is the job of the artist to be at the forefront of algorithm change, of "explicitly embed[ding] better values into our algorithms" [34] as Cathy O'Neil puts it, can easily override what artists do best – translate and misuse materials and processes that lie outside of their immediate understanding and control, given that artists draw on disciplines and professional knowledges without either being experts in these fields, or being willing to invest in them socially. This is why the notions of acting stupid and creative misuse are equally important as technical understanding here, or rather – certainly, as in the case of O'Connell – why misuse *presupposes* technical and social understanding and political commitment, and therefore why there is no misuse without technical understanding and research. Thus, the job of the artist is not simply to expand the skill range of the digital technician, even if technical understanding and immersion is paramount; it is to think a new relationship between art and technology by first denaturalizing the technosystem's claims to creativity. In this respect, we can outline four categories of analysis and practice that describe the intersection of theory, tech-knowledge, and artistic techniques of denaturalization (stupidity, misuse, comedic misunderstanding, etc.) in O'Connell's work.

1) The investigation of everyday functional processes, systems, tools, of the technosystem infrastructure, so as to

---

[33] Critical Art Ensemble, ibid, p137

[34] Cathy O'Neil, *Weapons of Math Destruction: How Big Data Increases Inequality and Threatens Democracy*, Crown, Penguin Random House, New York, 2016, p204

locate anomalies and aporias and produce alternative accounts and interpretations.

2) The misuse of, and deliberate misunderstanding of, technical and functional processes, systems, and tools, in order to create a dysfunctional, denaturalizing gap between user and technology.

3) The invention of seemingly innovative but 'pointless' (stupid) services, objects, processes utilizing everyday found materials and scenarios, in a kind of over-identification with neoliberal entrepreneurialism.

4) The presentation and use of data and found materials (electronic and object-based readymades) as the basis for critical research.

All four points are in a sense inseparable in O'Connell's practice, or least overlap. But nevertheless, they point to where the intersection of the comedic (stupidity) and the technical and technological lies in his work: in a kind of homing in on, and exposure of, the concealed human judgements and limited predictive outcomes programmed into software 'scripts' and their technologies. Over the past ten years he has intervened in, and misused, a range of municipal surveillance or monitoring systems and commercial delivery systems: car registration recognition and traffic jam image technologies, online ordering technologies, online parcel tracking technology, supermarket checkout technology, security camera technology, predictive text and audio recording, and parking fine detection technology. Each engagement by O'Connell with these technologies involves a disruptive, mischievous, investigative, or counter-intuitive use of each system. This generates in some instances a simple and humorous Turing-type test on 'service technology', as in his repeated use of supermarket chain Sainsbury's self-checkout machines over a three-month period in Brighton and London to 'buy nothing' (each receipt for £0.00 saying: "Thank you for your visit. Please let us know how we did.");[35] in others, a hard-grind pursuit of empirical research into the ways in which privatized technologies fleece the unguarded (as in his 'sousveillance' investigation, *Contra-Invention* [2010] into the overzealous activity of Brighton Council's traffic wardens through downloading publicly available images of the cars, which in some instances reveal the reflection of the officer who captured the image in the car's windscreen);[36] and in some cases the humorous collision between the high claims for the technical veracity of artificial intelligence (AI) voice recording and the actualities of colloquial speech and semantics, as in the AI transcription of an extended remote studio conversation between O'Connell and his artist colleague Tomasz Madajczak, during the Covid lockdown, in *NoSpace* (2021).[37] Indeed, the humour of the transcription lies in how misattribution through the weird off-the-wall predictive text function creates a perfect storm of technical and artistic stupidity, as if O'Connell was staging the unregulated

---

[35] For the published results see Micheál O'Connell / Mocksim, *Less*, Mocksim Arts/Services, Brighton, 2014

[36] See Micheál O'Connell / Mocksim, *Contra-Invention*, Brighton Biennial, Brighton, 2010. "Just as [council traffic wardens] made records of offending vehicles, they could be captured in the act of issuing fines on my mobile device (Nokia 6500c and Nokia 6700c-1). Also I began deliberately manoeuvring my way into the field of view in an attempt to appear in their photographs. The phone handset played a part in these ruses. It was better to appear in conversation making a call, distracted and not loitering. And the knack of capturing [council traffic wardens] in action while the device was held to my ear in pretend dialogue amounted to another new craft skill comparable with the methods used by street photographers in the past – not wanting to be noticed by their subjects." (Micheál O'Connell, *Art as 'Artificial Stupidity'*, PhD thesis, University of Sussex, 2016, p104).
One extraordinary fact about car ownership and use is how little people drive their cars; see Paul Barter, '"Cars are parked 95% of the time". Let's check!', Reinventing Parking website, available at: https://bit.ly/2FO9wkr

[37] Tomasz Madajczak and Micheál O'Connell, *NoSpace*, Mocsim Arts/Services, Brighton, 2021

idiocy of artists when left to their own devices. Or, as if O'Brien, Samuel Beckett, and Georges Perec were co-authoring *The Life of the Young Artist as an Ass* as the basis for a Saturday Night Live sketch. Sections are worth quoting in full:

Tomasz: It feels that I'm trying to move, but I'm kind of

Micheál: Stuck yeah. That must be frequent enough green feeling I have had that to where I can't seem to go into the next space or just, just go on for ages why I kind of want to go on the dreamers and allowing me to progress. Yeah.[38]

Tomasz: How, how is it possible to live life like I'm what what what what life would be like. No, no I agree

Micheál: And

Tomasz: So coming back to the space and yeah, and questioning that to what we are doing and what's what's happening.[39]

Tomasz: Yes, I was going to tell us we started class

Micheál: I forgot the sink isn't

Tomasz: Seen pieces of that really annoying me, a basically aesthetically annoying me. I have no idea of what you're doing here, and its kind of whenever I looked at out the pieces of just, it shouldn't be me.

Micheál: Show me

Tomasz: Show me give you some food

Micheál: Oh, can't you just take them out

---

[38] Tomasz Madajczak and Micheál O'Connell, ibid, p60
[39] Tomasz Madajczak and Micheál O'Connell, ibid, p66

Tomasz: I will

Micheál: Always say yeah yeah yeah, I get those in [40]

Micheál: It goes against my instincts, but it doesn't go against your instincts because you you you do enjoy Kraftwerk

Tomasz: But then I enjoy even when I can find a way of making something really powerful

Micheál: Like because because this what we're doing now is we're trying to solve this problem is is labor is his craft scale is is taking its using knowledge that we both have experienced with. So in a sense of we came to an elegant solution that involve just going and that would, that wouldn't be the work involved the work involved is all this isn't it.

Tomasz: Okay, maybe we'll try [41]

Micheál: I don't like the idea of covering things up as they're part of the workings either, but we're just gently hiding things

Tomasz: Yeah. I think I'm starting small piece of paper like because it's elegant and simple.

Micheál: Yeah.

Tomasz: And the tracing paper of the lights. It's kind of I like the fact that they need to be here, but the we can try to put a veil over the veil

Micheál: A mask it's all about masks. These there's no tomatoes.

---

[40] Tomasz Madajczak and Micheál O'Connell, ibid, p85
[41] Tomasz Madajczak and Micheál O'Connell, ibid, p91-92

Tomasz: Lettuce mask the space.[42]

Micheál: So may be so you were talking out in the sea. And how you see that is extremely different to being an Asian a big room. The other somehow bringing that experience inside

Tomasz: When that's why again. I like the idea of the camera obscura because it would project the outside, inside

Micheál: Yeah.

Tomasz: And we would be inside experiencing the inside the way inside these but with the notion of terrorists outside, which is kind of which is something we tend to forget when we visit in art studio with Vista Gallery, we get into a gallery and and we look for something that is in the garden, outside the gallery. Yeah yeah[43]

The inanity and hilarity of the exchanges not only reflect O'Connell's willingness to expose himself and Madajczak through a third party – AI – (in the greater interest of thinking stupidity), to the preposterousness of unguarded studio artistic talk, as if machine intelligence here malevolently and systematically transforms what is normally on the verge of unintelligibility into complete idiocy. But it also exposes machinic intelligence to a shattering shaming itself: the machine does not know what it is talking about. By pushing the speech recognition technology semantically further than it's usually asked to perform, the predictive text function blows a fuse – those crazy artists, with their crazy concepts – creating a strange de-semanticized language that further exposes the empty efficiency of digital intellectual labour. At one level, this kind of 'system interference' draws on Dada and post-Oulipo aleatory visual and literary practice, what is known these days as e-office literature or Flarf poetry or writing. Most of this work derives from the collocation of disparate

---

[42] Tomasz Madajczak and Micheál O'Connell, ibid, p98-99
[43] Tomasz Madajczak and Micheál O'Connell, ibid, p113-114

semantic materials of contemporary digital exchange, such as in chat rooms, Twitter, Google, official e-office communications and tech-jargon. Revelling in its collaging of disparate linguistic elements taken out of context, the resulting semantic disjunction of the writing teases out the frail self-justifying order of management discourse.[44] O'Connell's own 'semantic adjustments', however, cover different artistic and epistemological ground. Indifferent to any unexpected poetic resonances or unexpected critical encounters in the spirit of Surrealism's 'Exquisite Corpse', the relentless self-exposure of stupidity in *NoSpace* draws out one of the key aspects of all Turing tests: the incapacity of machine intelligence to generate convincing abductive thought patterns. That is, patterns of analysis and association that bypass predictive calculations and pregiven pathways, in order to 'think on the job' and create new connections and links or unpredictable avenues for conversation and new research. As Charles Sanders Peirce argued as the modern founder of abductive thought (although Immanuel Kant and Sigmund Freud and psychoanalytic method run him a close second) there is no creative advance in knowledge without 'critical intuition';[45] and no making of 'new patterns' without breaking with 'received patterns'. Machine intelligence, thus, always comes up short abductively, given the reliance of computing algorithmically on homophily and retroactive probability. This is because homophily and retroactive probability are short cuts to understanding as a result of their betting on preestablished associations to establish relevant and predictable connections, as opposed to the grasping of meaning through a reliance on those complex modes of sociality, historical

---

[44] For discussion of Flarf poetry and post-digital 'e-office writing', see Jasper Bernes, *The Work of Art in the Age of Deindustrialization*, Stanford University Press, Stanford, 2017

[45] Charles Sanders Peirce, *The Essential Peirce*, two volumes, ed. Peirce Edition Project, Indiana University Press, Indiana, 1992 and 1998. For a discussion of Peirce and Freud and abduction, see John Roberts, *The Necessity of Errors*, Verso, London and New York, 2011

understanding, and causal determination, that language infers and mobilizes.

Indeed, engaging with the meaning of the most basic of human conversations involves a huge amount of pre-embedded socialization and understanding of belief and intention (causal presuppositions) through extended natural language use on the part of participants and listeners – an emphasis on the interrelationship of meaning and context that is just unavailable to the inert, desocialized, biography-less language use of computers. It is no surprise therefore that some version of abductive thinking has become the new Holy Grail of AI, the qualitative transformation in machine intelligence that will truly mark the passage of humans into the posthuman and the would-be singularity – the interfusion of machines and bodies. Intelligence machines *can* become 'intelligent intelligence machines', the new AI advocates insist; nothing technically and scientifically suggests otherwise, for there is no reason not to believe that with the reverse engineering of the brain machines can replicate the abductive leaps in thinking and practice of humans. Consequently, abduction today has become the major site of ideological conflict about the value and meaning of machine intelligence, the posthuman and technological advance, a site of fundamental contestation between the meaning of being human and being posthuman.

For the defenders of machine-centred abduction, the de facto establishment of technological limits on the expansion of machine intelligence, therefore, denies the meaning of what humans might become as a result of machine intelligence and also what machine intelligence might become as an extension of human invention. As Reza Negarestani argues: "The opposition between the possibility of a thinking machine and the actuality of the human agent should be exposed as a false dichotomy..."[46] There is no technological impediment, in principle, to machine-based abduction, because

---

[46] Reza Negarestani, *Intelligence and Spirit*, Urbanomic, Falmouth and Sequence Press, New York, 2018, p119

there are no preset limits on how science and technology might extend the human into the machinic. But presumably, tech companies don't want their future supercomputers to break off from their analysis of stress fracture patterns during bridge construction modelling, to say: 'I just can't go on, this is tedious beyond all belief, I need to get back to my poetry.' They no doubt would want their machines to remain 'happy, efficient idiots', and continue working, as opposed to being 'unhappy inefficient thinkers', like most humans, intent on sabotaging, refusing, or qualifying what is required of them. So, whatever, computers might achieve in terms of free-will, human-like semantic complexity, context-determinate self-reflection, and socialized agency, the question of what 'thinking' is is a fateful one, insofar as an increase in computational power may at some point replicate the abductive creativity of humans, but the very increase in computational power may also actually undermine what makes human abductive processes the non-predictive arrangements they are; that is, their reliance on 'stupidity' or guesswork to get to where thinking may take place. Making machines properly intelligently stupid, human stupid, rather than simply stupid, computationally stupid, may in fact destroy what makes biologically determined consciousness the exceptional thing it is. To a certain extent Negarestani recognizes this. Although the transformation and expansion of the human-machine interface/integration cannot be predicted on the basis of initial human conditions, posthuman technological divergence from a biological model of the human, as *freely* divergent, is a myth: "...the main issue here is that there is simply no such thing as an emergent behaviour divergent from initial conditions in an unconfined or unbounded manner. There is no guarantee of uniform divergence from or convergence toward initial conditions."[47] Negarestani, then, acknowledges that there is something deeper at stake than technological divergence sweeping away the assumed transcendental structures of consciousness that prop up the humanist subject. He asks: "What kinds of basic capacities must

[47] Reza Negarestani, ibid, p99

these [artificial general intelligence, AGI] agents have in order to support complex schemas of self-conception and self-revision?"[48] What continuity between the human and the human-machinic makes the lives of human-machines viable? Indeed, this is precisely the question that anti-divergence defenders of abduction ask.

The content of what a bounded technological divergence might be has become crucial to a range of recent positions on the technosystem and the reengineering of the human that see abduction as central to averting AI's expanded computational assimilation of abductive thinking and the idea that radical divergence is inevitable and therefore better. This is the logic of technological 'winners' that even Negarestani's leftism buys into, despite his resistance to technological inevitablism. A number of recent writers though (in particular, Andrew Feenberg, Yuk Hui, Slavoj Žižek, and Erik J. Larson, whom I will look at here) see abductive thinking, or something like it, not just as the creative space for better thinking that open system computational logic can replicate and facilitate in the interests of 'problem solving', but also as the basis of a resistive subjectivity that challenges what technical expansion and the dissolution of the human-technology-*technē* interspace actually is creatively, and therefore what abductive thinking can meaningfully accomplish, its emancipatory potential. All writers identify abduction with the critique of the fetishized model of computational intelligence; all see computation's statistical model of induction as a covert positivism and essentially anti-theoretical; and all link abductive thinking (or something like it) to the innovative potential of a creative rationality attached to the non-probabilistic, non-predictive and contingent. In these terms, Feenberg and Larson attach abduction principally to the technical and social struggle inside the technosystem to remove the vast weight of enumerative, computational induction from the foreground of scientific research programmes, scientific education and the delimited choices and experiences driving digital

---

[48] Reza Negarestani, ibid, p139

platforms and the everyday capitalist life. In this respect Feenberg connects the broader popular aspects of this struggle to how abduction links the amateur and abductive thinking to the spirit of 'citizen science'. "The abductive leap is not formally rational but nevertheless is recognized as essential to rational thought. Both professional and lay actors are capable of abductions that transform the technical environment."[49] On this basis we might assume that Myles na Gopaleen's 'man of knowledge' would be Feenberg's ideal abductive thinker: "the identification of unsuspected potentials leads to a reconceptualization of the object to better serve new usages".[50] Larson takes a similar 'citizen science' type route: because enumerative computation cannot produce embedded, contextually determined knowledge, it cannot produce the levels of reflexive knowledge – reasoning from events to their causes – that abductive thinking requires. What are needed, therefore, to push back against the scientific demotion of non-computational knowledge are"wide-ranging and disparate research agendas to encourage creative hypotheses and spur discovery"[51] based on broad participation. For Larson this means that: abduction "captures the insight that much of our everyday reasoning is a kind of detection work…Without a prior abductive step, inductions are blind, and deductions are equally useless."[52] Larson's and Feenberg's priority, then, working within the broad field of social constructivism, ally abduction to the technical priorities that I highlighted earlier in my discussion of Wendy Chun and the struggle against homophily: this is the technical and social push against enumerative computation, in order to free up a popular space for the critical transformation of the digital landscape and the denaturalization of predatory technologies. As

---

[49] Andrew Feenberg, *Technosystem: The Social Life of Reason*, Harvard University Press, Cambridge Mass. and London, 2017, p182
[50] Andrew Feenberg, ibid, p182
[51] Erik J. Larson, *The Myth of Artificial Intelligence: Why Computers Can't Think the Way We Do*, The Belknap Press of Harvard University Press, Cambridge Mass. and London, 2021, p267
[52] Erik J. Larson, ibid, p161

such this involves a practical consolidation and development of the social implications of model three of our models of 'system interference': the widening of 'participation interests' of workers and citizens inside the technosystem. In the broad continuum of specialist and non-specialist participants, the knowledge and experience of workers and citizens living and working inside the technical systems of platform capitalism becomes an integral part of a wider set of political demands about the limit of market democracy and its increasing fatalistic alliance with posthuman inevitabilism. As Feenberg says: "To create a place for agency, technical citizens must struggle to overcome [computational inevitability] and achieve consciousness of the contingency of the technical domain."[53] Thus, in this emergent 'constructionist' space, the opposition between "irrational society and rational technosystem invoked by technocratic ideology"[54] (Elon Musk, Peter Thiel, Mark Zuckerberg) has no validity.

In Hui's and Žižek's engagement with the abductive question, the link between abductive thinking and a project of public and civil constructionism doesn't operate in the same way, even if both writers give a similar kind of consideration to the normative dimensions of the critique of technology under capitalism. What preoccupies Hui in contrast to Feenberg and Larson is the productive link between abductive thinking and the context-determined, causal-sensitive conditions of judgement and understanding that define human learning and creativity. In this he is explicit about needing to defend the exceptionalism of human abductive thinking and a philosophical account of a (critical) transcendentalism. "For a computer, the judgement of a proposition is nothing but the technicization of knowledge, whereas for a human being, the logical operation has to be based on experience itself. This is precisely the motivation of

---

[53] Andrew Feenberg, ibid, p59
[54] Andrew Feenberg, ibid, p59

transcendental phenomenology."[55] In these terms human abductive thinking is the necessary basis of the de-technicization of knowledge – of creative guesswork – that is needed to generate new interobjective relations inside the technosystem. (Interobjectivity refers to the materialization of the internal and external relations of objects, reflected in the fact that an ensemble of tools can become a system of increasing complexity, determining and concretizing the outcomes of intersubjective use.) So, in these terms, abduction is the means by which people's relationship to the meaning of digital objects inside the technosystem is mediated not by (hidden and manipulative) indicative pathways that flatter to deceive, but by the creative 'leaps' and disruptions of individual/group users. The technical decisions that order current interobjective relations – the 'pseudo-'we's' of digital life – are disrupted and made available to reflexive use and reattachment to real world divisions, solidarities, and agency.

For Hui, though, there is something more significant in the identification of abduction (critical intuition) with the questioning and testing of the human-machine symbiosis, something philosophically and politically more demanding than the technical/scientific remodeling of systems and technological use values. Constructivism as a project, for Hui, still remains attached to a technocratic futurism even if it is defined by 'alternative' technologies, 'citizen science' and popular participation, and is opposed to full posthuman technological immersion. The relationship between humans and technology therefore is still to be defined in ways that shift the overall axis of technology away from what he calls planetary technological determinism; that is, the belief that better technologies (even those based on an abductive rationality) can secure human progress, particularly as alternative technologies of progress are still defined and shaped by capitalist accumulation. Hence, the relationship between abduction,

---

[55] Yuk Hui, *On the Existence of Digital Objects*, University of Minnesota Press, Minneapolis and London, 2016, p206

technology and the technosystem needs another kind of positional and analytic thinking, in which the development of an abductive-centred relationship between interobjectivity and intersubjectivity redefine rationality and progress as an open and reflexive relationship with technologies and their users in the plural, rather than simply continuing to expand the current technosystem through the assimilation of non-determinate models of artificial intelligence. For Hui, this shift can only be achieved by placing art, as the crucible of the indeterminate and the 'incalculable', in critical relationship to technology. In other words, art becomes the privileged site of abductive thinking and practice. "A scientific hypothesis is a claim that something is necessary before it is proven so. Art commits to a necessity of a different nature. Necessity in art is not about demonstrating the rational (i.e. deduction or induction) but rather a process of rationalization with or without an axiomatic foundation. Art cannot be founded on science."[56] However, this is not adaptation of late-Romantic expressivism and the practical subordination of science and technology to the 'aesthetic life', and the acceptance of the anti-rational or irrational with truth. On the contrary, abduction or critical intuition here serves what Hui calls the non-rational, that is those reflexive processes that sustain the open-endedness of reason but are not reducible to the probabilistic and axiomatic ground of science as a calculable system of knowledge and prediction. "Science starts with a demonstrable ground, while art starts with a groundless ground..."[57] Thus, under the abductive demands of this groundless ground, art acts precisely in the interests of the 'unknown' and unpredictable, which in turn means that objectively – potentially – it has the capacity to act in the interests of producing a new human-technology relation (interobjectivity/intersubjectivity) inside the technosystem, *but not on technology's or the technosystem's terms*. So, there is a bigger metaphysical claim here regarding the human-technology relation than advanced by the constructivist position.

---

[56] Yuk Hui, *Art and Cosmotechnics*, e-flux/University of Minnesota Press, Minneapolis, 2021, p115
[57] Yuk Hui, ibid, p124

Hui writes: "Thinking must recognize that the post-metaphysical world no longer restricts imagination to any well-defined and articulated transcendence, like Platonic form or Christian God, nor does it return imagination to a primitive wildness. Rather it establishes a new rationalization, with and through technology. This new rationalization doesn't confine itself to techno-logos or 'Occidental rationality', but rather re-grounds technology by resituating it in broader realities."[58] That is, the non-rational and abductive therefore provide the means of denaturalizing the claim that the instrumental rationalization of 'rational nature' is the source of all value. 'Rational nature' in Kant's sense, can through art's abductive powers produce new directions and frameworks for science and technology that radically disconnect technological progress from its governing logico-capital reality, and the elite and predatory pathways under which progress currently labours: the geo-engineering of the poor (in the interests of a new social genetics and the complete alignment of desire with the market), the biotechnical enhancement of the middle class and the rich, and the industrial 'conquest' of outer space.

There is also a 'bigger metaphysical' claim outlined in Žižek's recent writing on the human-technology relation, although art is not one of his concerns. Like Hui he focuses on what the fetishization of technical necessity and the advancement of artificial intelligence forgets, in its posthuman divergence from the human, thereby narrowing what human 'rational nature' enables as a condition of human flourishing. However, rather than drawing attention specifically to abductive thinking or critical intuition as central to this, he develops his own version of the non-rational: the positive power of human imperfection and lack, or what he calls the constitutive role of limitation in being human. "Since our – humanity's – 'highest' achievements are rooted in our very ultimate limitations (failure, mortality, and the concomitant sexuality), i.e., in what we cannot but experience as the obstacle to our 'higher' spiritual existence, the idea that this 'higher' level can

---

[58] Yuk Hui, ibid, p125-26

survive without what prevents its full actualization, is an illusion…"[59] In other words, what the computational rationality of the technosystem threatens is how this constitutive deficiency of the human actually defines and regulates the pleasures of forgetting, loss, ignorance, error, of not succeeding, as a condition of sustaining desire.[60] Thus, these would-be weaknesses do not constitute the unforgiving failure of the human to achieve the completed rationalization of its 'rational nature', but constitute the positive means by which reason and desire are produced and a non-dominative rationality enabled. In this sense the dream of full technological immersion is to propose the opposite: to transform the human into the monstrously 'fully born', the subject who knows no loss, no forgetting as the reconfiguration of knowing, no non-rational detours, as a condition of his/her/their exit from biophysical inconsistency and breakdown. This is why it is precisely the purported obstacles to the full rationalization of 'rational nature' that secures freedom, given that, without the negotiation and renegotiation of obstacles, freedom becomes an indeterminate end-state and self-fulfilling teleology. The potentiality that inheres in the obstacle and its overcoming dissolves: "…if we take away the obstacle the very potential thwarted by this obstacle dissipates." [61] In other words, the technocratic posthuman dream of non-mediation is a form of false rationalization, in as much it assumes that divergence from the limits of the merely human is coeval with emancipation as the end of all superfluous biological and cognitive constraints. Machines are held to possess unrestricted possibilities; humans are held to have a limited potentiality. But: "…what if directly getting what we want [technological immortality, the cessation of subjective and physical pain] desublimates what we get and thus renders it

---

[59] Slavoj Žižek, *Hegel in a Wired Brain*, Bloomsbury Academic, London, 2020, p136
[60] With specific reference to the ontological and epistemological status of the error in relation to this question, see John Roberts, *The Necessity of Errors*, Verso, London and New York, 2011
[61] Slavoj Žižek, ibid, p137

worthless?...[in overcoming] the experience of the unbearable loss of mediation/detour [finitude]:we get the desired thing itself, but without the network of mediations which make it desirable?"[62] We might say, then, the law of constitutive deficiency and limitation is the key to the non-probabilistic horizons of creativity – the thing that makes human exceptionalism ultimately incompatible with reverse brain engineering.

The four positions outlined above are not anti-AI and computational science; they are all careful to place their critiques of digital capitalism internal to the critique of the anti-technology position. In this they all clearly situate themselves outside of the human-technology *duality*. Humans are embedded in technical relations. However, the authors do recognize that the current defenders of computational science have a fundamental case to answer when it comes to technology and emancipation under present global conditions. Abductive reason or critical intuition, the non-rational, and constitutive deficiency all mark out the aporias, claustrophobia and teleological crisis of computational capitalism in the stage of its Promethean death drive. In this there is a shared insistence that the critical struggle inside the technosystem must be one in which the thought of the exception, failure, and loss has to define producers and users abductive leap beyond homophily and retroactive probability. Thus, it is no surprise that some artists who take the technical interrogation of the technosystem seriously, such as Micheál O'Connell, make it their business to work through the non-rational potentiality of art as the basis of this interrogation. This is why we might place O'Connell's 'stupidity' and misuse of machines and technical processes more broadly under the ethics of abduction. Just as Žižek does not inflate constitutive deficiency into a constitutive and comforting humanness, O'Connell does not inflate 'thinking stupidity' into a comforting eco-conservationism or a vision of the future as DIY knick-knackery. Rather, his humorous entanglement in the 'reason of machines' – his understanding and deflation of the

---

[62] Slavoj Žižek, ibid, p142

machine's imputed magic – produces a negative exposure of computation by making machines 'give up' their repressed idiocy, producing a judgement not on machines as such, but on their programmers and masters. In this respect O'Connell's 'thinking stupidity' and critical misuse works in two directions simultaneously: to show how the human calculations and 'scripts' of machines and their novel efficiencies are easily opened up to comedic non-compliance; and how the artist, in a kind of complicity with this relentless drive of machinic novelty, in breaking the spell of technological naturalization, needs to produce a technological encounter or technical intervention that will arrest the interest of the spectator; that will, in short, demonstrate a degree of inventiveness in keeping with the life of machines and their producers themselves. There is a sense, then, that the artist himself or herself, in order to 'keep up' technically, is caught up in the drive to innovation as the ground of making sense of the technosystem. Simply shouting at machines or throwing them off cliffs is to end any worthwhile dialogue you might have with technology – and art.

## Chapter 3: Impotentiality and Obtrusion

This attentiveness to machinic novelty thus requires for our purposes a shift, more expressly, into political economy. Technological innovation is the irredeemable horizon of capital accumulation and technical embeddedness. Without innovation, local and generic, contingent and structural, capitalist production falls into crisis and decline; the very logic of inter-enterprise competition is the logic of technical innovation. To get ahead capitalistically is to innovate; to create new consumers is to make visible and convincing the link between product innovation and necessity, the new, and an advance in pleasure and satisfaction. Consequently, from the perspective of the artist and theorist, to get 'entangled' in technology is in a sense to get entangled in the stupidity of its contrivances and false teleologies. Indeed, as Sianne Ngai argues in her engaging and astute, *Theory of the Gimmick: Aesthetic Judgment and Capitalist Form* (2020)[63] it is precisely the logic of the gimmick that haunts and shapes the capitalist development of technology – for the neutral notion of 'innovation' with all its rationally arrived assumptions about progress, fails to capture the desperation and bad faith of technological development, its irrational attachment to the worst best option, if the worst best can guarantee consumers and profits. Cars could have been far safer, better designed, and ecologically more efficient if not for the reliance on the massive profits derived from the expansion of the fossil fuel economy, which continues today with the power that the American car industry retains over fuel efficiency and eco standards.[64] This touches on the importance of

---

[63] Sianne Ngai, *Theory of the Gimmick: Aesthetic Judgment and Capitalist Form*, The Belknap Press of Harvard University Press, Cambridge Mass. and London, 2020

[64] See Andreas Malm and the Zetkin Collective, *White Skin, Black Fuel: On the Danger of Fossil Fascism*, Verso, London and New York, 2021. See also: Paris Marx, *Road to Nowhere: What Silicon Valley Gets*

the two key pillars of modern political economy: the vast production of waste and pollution as the driver of renewal and the *technical* market solutions to fundamental structural problems; and – outside of the expansion of mass markets – capitalism's powerful anti-sumptuary logic; that is, the fact that only a small part of the economy now actually satisfies basic needs, while the largest part, the anti-sumptuary part, meets, produces and intensifies diverse desires (the growth in the postwar libidinal economy) and the luxury and surplus consumption of the middle class and the rich. As Gernot Böhme notes, once the meeting of basic needs is superseded as a condition of 'growth', "surplus consumption is no longer a transcending of the sphere of necessity, and still less a transition to the realm of freedom. Instead, by evolving desires human beings exactly fulfil the necessities of the capitalist economic system…human beings transform their system of needs in order to satisfy the requirement of capitalist development…"[65] This is precisely where Ngai sites her theory of the gimmick: in the forced or strained push of innovation across the technological divide between mass markets and the anti-sumptuary logic of the modern libidinal economy and its need for relentless innovation and difference. As she says, as a result of this forcing, the gimmick is radically unstable, given that it suffers invariably from bad timing, that is from being "too old or too new"[66] in respect of its claims for innovation and novelty. "Under- or overperforming with respect to [the] historical norm, [the gimmick] strikes us as technologically backward or just as problematically advanced..."[67]

---

*Wrong about the Future of Transportation,* Verso, London and New York, 2022, for a critique of the ecological claims of the electric car, given the massive global expansion of mineral extraction needed to support the privatized substitution of the internal combustion engine with electric power. Marx calls for an integrated socialized transport system combining a mixture of low-tech and high-tech technologies.

[65] Gernot Böhme, *Critique of Aesthetic Capitalism,* Mimesis International, Milan, 2017, p12

[66] Sianne Ngai, *Theory of the Gimmick: Aesthetic Judgment and Capitalist Form,* ibid, p2

[67] Sianne Ngai, ibid, p2

Indeed, as "overrated devices that strike us as working too little (labor-saving tricks) but also as working too hard (strained efforts to get our attention). In each case we refer to the aesthetically suspicious object as a "contrivance," an ambiguous term equally applicable to ideas, techniques and things." [68] The gimmick is, consequently, for Ngai not only capitalism's "most successful aesthetic category"[69] (in Böhme's sense of mature capitalism as a *self*-aestheticizing system) – in as much as it mobilizes the desire for novelty as a solution to the maintenance of subject's affective attachment to capitalist reproduction – but also the unstable evidence of the false promise of that very novelty. Indeed, evidence of the bloatedness of capitalism's anti-sumptuary logic; that is, depending on the limits of one's investment or not in the pleasures of capitalist superfluity. Indeed, the pleasures of the gimmick in the anti-sumptuary economy easily flips into its opposite once the perception of the idea of the gimmick as trying too hard is allied to a sense of luxuriant wastefulness and stupefying inefficiency. The transformation of the gimmick in this way is beautifully illustrated on Gwyneth Paltrow's *Goop* site[70] – that is, beautifully illustrated for those viewers who possess a modicum of ironic indifference to the consumerist hierarchy the site seeks to impose through its utterly unreflexive presentation of luxuriant beauty and 'good design'. The listed objects, which are largely pitched at rich young women, are all resplendent in their smooth gimmickiness, and are all attached to enticingly absurd high prices, and as such, are all deliciously and comically overdefined by their (useless) luxuriousness:

Double-Sided Wand Vibrator. The ultimate intimate massager. $98.00

---

[68] Sianne Ngai, ibid, p1

[69] Sianne Ngai, ibid, p2

[70] See products at: https://goop.com

Date Night Set. Rabbit vibrator and vibrating penis ring for couple play. $199.00

Zeitgeist Baby Carrier. Cashmere, organic cotton, and mulberry silk. $787.00

Ultraplush Self-Heating G-Spot Vibrator. The perfect curve for exploring your G-spot. $95.00

Rainbow Mat. Ease tension in the body with infrared heat and hot gemstones. $1,999.00

Skyview Wellnesss Table Lamp. Designed to bring the biological benefits of natural light indoors. $750.00

Red Light Face Mask. From the much-loved sauna experts this easy-to-wear mask combines red and near-infrared light for powerful skin-care benefits. $299.00

Luxury Towel Warmer. For that fresh warm, straight-out-of-the-dryer feel. $160.00

Pelvic Clock Exercise Device. A simple tool for lower back flexibility, hip mobility, and alignment. $84.00

Ngai would no doubt see these items as the perfected logic of trying too hard in the luxury gimmick stakes, insofar as the utility of the products are drowned out by their ridiculous superfluity. They are gimmicks that are "ostentatiously unworthy", [71] and therefore given our working analytic category of 'stupidity' in this short book are evidence, of what we might say, utter 'stupidity' – the kind of stupidity that Ronell defines as the kind that purveys a "self-assured assertiveness, [that] mutes just about everything that would seek to disturb its impervious hierarchies".[72] Ngai doesn't

---

[71] Sianne Ngai, ibid, p9

[72] Avital Ronell, *Stupidity*, ibid, p3

discuss the link between stupidity and the gimmick, but her writing certainly provides us with additional cognitive and technical resources in order to think the relationship between the lives of machines, the exigencies of capitalist innovation, and the performative role of the artist as a thinking, non-compliant defaulter from computational reason. For what is paramount here is, as I mentioned above, how the artist functions inside the technosystem as someone who is no less caught up in the dynamic of capitalist innovation as the gimmick-driven programmer or designer. This is not a crude mimicry of the market but a cognitive necessity. O'Connell in this sense *performs and tests* his own capture by this submission to technological novelty. This is why I'm happy to use Ngai's notion of the gimmick here, but nevertheless there is a strong sense in which the artist's reliance on the 'gimmick' is quite different from the technical gimmicks and gimmick objects that determine the interobjective and intersubjective relations of the tech-consumer landscape and AI technosystem. That is, artists of any worth do not produce gimmicks in a calculated first-order sense as a means to persuade and cajole, or astonish. Thus, contrary to much conventional – and even radical – art history Duchamp's *Fountain* and the early unassisted readymades, for example, are not gimmicks that are conscious attempts to entice, but cognitive and material ruptures in the patterns of capitalist acculturation and mimetic naturalization associated with traditional forms of aesthetic judgement and traditional artistic skills. Gimmicks, then, as they inhabit the object world of the technosystem as would-be creative flashpoints (look at that!) do not set out to denaturalize, even if in some instances they seek to persuade us that if we purchase a particular object or service it might improve our working life or open up new pathways to creativity outside of our workplace (as risibly was the case in the promotion of the first generation of smartphones). The gimmick of the smartphone was in the end really only the novelty of being connected to the market 24/7. Thus, it is only artists who produce gimmicks in the manner of the technical object world – the kind of artists today, indeed, who are associated with the vast swathes of AI image programming, such as the asinine CloudPainter and DeepDream vision programmes and their epigones, and dim-witted, skateboarding robot painters – who might be said to be artists who produce gimmicks in the sense Ngai outlines. Hence, there is an important distinction around novelty and technology in art that needs to be clarified here in order to make a substantive claim about O'Connell's immanent critique of computational reason and, therefore, what his art is precisely not engaged in. This is the confusion about art's technical and technological emergence. It is not good enough simply to say that, given art is already emergent technically, already embedded in interobjective and intersubjective relations, any old AI will do. This is the idea under the posthuman dictates of the technosystem that it is the programmed computer that calls the shots. This is the shift from the modernist and avant-garde notion of the human-with-the-machine to the notion of the human-*as*-a-machine. [73] Under this shift, what becomes a conformist priority is the idea of the artist as a technical facilitator of technological innovation; the artist no longer defines a possible creative/critical relationship *with* the machine, but simply submits to its would-be 'creative' efficiency in the interests of the widest possible definition of what an artist-as-the-prosthetic extension of computational reason might be. Indeed, once human abduction is 'out of the picture' here, the computational system takes over, providing access to the realm of art-machine production 'democratically' for all. Entry level knowledge and skills are practically zero; minor shifts in iterations of a system or pattern (the ordered generative image) are an artistic priority in an endless process of mutation, which in some instances can be

---

[73] In the 1920s László Moholy-Nagy gave a forthright avant-garde defence of the artist-machine interface: "This is our century – technology, machine, socialism. Make your peace with it. Shoulder its task." From 'Constructivism and the proletariat', *MA* (May 1922), collected in Richard Kostelanetz ed. *Moholy-Nagy*, Documentary Monographs in Modern Art, Allen Lane, London, 1974, p185

reprogrammed by users who dislike previous iterations.[74] Thus, the continuous adaptation of technological innovation is the key to this transformation, objectively allying visual production with the commercial post-professional (that is post-theoretical) cultural agendas of the big tech companies and the need for consumers to continually purchase new software to 'play the game'; indeed, the game of participating in the distracting, enticing, spectacular work of the gimmick. Consequently, the big-tech cultural adaptation of AI is more than just the neutral presentation of new technical innovation and technologies. As Joanna Zylinska stresses: technical innovation and new technological tools become "an active agent in shaping tastes, regulating market and defining what counts as mainstream visuality. The work of art is therefore not just mechanically reproduced but also algorithmically produced."[75] That is, by those with access to the hardware and software. In this way the governing reliance on machine intelligence, as the means by which cultural democracy is presently secured by the many, subtly reinforces what Günther Anders calls the inculcation of shame in front of machines, the shame that comes with thinking that critical theory and cultural negation, and human-machine creativity can lead to nothing but impotence when faced with the greater efficiency of computational machine intelligence. Anders calls this the "curtailing [of] oneself in the attempt to 'measure up to a machine'."[76] "...it is machines that now [only] count as

---

[74] See Thomas Nail's discussion of the ordered and disordered generative and artistic image and literary text in *Theory of the Image*, Oxford University Press, Oxford, 2019

[75] Joanna Zylinska, *AI Art: Machine Visions and Warped Dreams*, Open Humanities Press, London, 2020, p69

[76] Günther Anders, 'On Promethean Shame', in Christopher John Müller, *Prometheanism: Technology, Digital Culture and Human Obsolescence*, Rowman & Littlefield International, London and New York, 2016, p49. Originally published as 'Über Prometheische Scham', in Günther Anders, *Die Antiquiertheit des Menschen 1: Über die Seele im Zeitalter der zweiten industriellen Revolution* [1956], C.H.Beck, Munich, 2002

'grown-up'."[77] Technological shame, or what Anders describes as Promethean shame, consists then in preferring what is made over the maker. This is much to do, he argues, with the fact that the production of machines appears to have no discernible producers (given that machines are partly produced by other machines) and therefore that machines are more "likely to be proof of one's own insufficiency than evidence of one's own power"[78] (as a producer; as a part of the collective workforce). The result is that humans, compelled to acknowledge the greater intellectual and efficient power of machines, feel shame *at not being a thing*. "Humans now acknowledge the superiority of things, bring themselves into line with them, and *welcome their own reification*."[79] The outcome is that the shame of insufficiency becomes attached to the burden of individuation. The notion of human exceptionalism – the 'malaise of uniqueness' – increasingly appears to be utterly superfluous and contrary to the shared life of machinic reproducibility and the joy of the same. In other words, individuation as the life of extra-machinic intelligence and creativity feels as if it is extraneous to living as part of a shared machine life, in which one's powers of creativity are matched up to the creativity of others as part of shared machinic consciousness.

The biotech development of AI feeds on and shapes this shame and these feelings of lack as a means of aligning the subject with the gift and support of computational power. The subject is taken up into the machine as a condition of surpassing human biophysical and cognitive insufficiency, a bit like the joyous submissiveness that supposedly accompanies Christian fundamentalist rapture. Thus, it is no surprise that AI art is fuelled by an anti-intellectual *ressentiment* and desire for immersive pleasure. The programmers and defenders of the new AI vision programs and robot 'painters' feel that a new stage of placid, post-critical visual immersiveness has arrived that excludes no one and no thing; all images, all data,

---

[77] Günther Anders, 'On Promethean Shame', ibid, p44
[78] Günther Anders, ibid, p33
[79] Günther Anders, ibid, p35

are open to an endless and playful interfusion. But as Zylinska says, the uncritical acceptance of "mild bemusement" soon begets the celebration of a "worryingly uncritical instrumentalism".[80] I would go further: the indulgence in the cheerful, turgid blandness of CloudPainter and DeepDream begets a sado-infantilism, in which 'pleasantness' and imbecilic niceness and a mild ersatz surrealist creepiness are suffused with an underlying threat of violence and fear. This is because these immersive, infantilizing pleasures of the image are far more insidious than the delight they create in producing feelings of uncanniness from the deep algorithmic mutation and convergence of images. That is, this technology of image immersion heightens and objectifies one of the key ideological mechanisms of the subject's adaptation to the neoliberal sensorium: faith in apophenia, the trusting of the pleasures taken in perceiving would-be meaningful patterns and connections between disconnected and random phenomena as revealing hidden truths, or what we know philosophically from Gottfried Leibniz as 'associative' thinking.[81] Associative thinking is what we might call 'non-educated' abduction, to transliterate a phrase from Fredric Jameson about conspiracy theory being a form of cognitive mapping for uneducated beginners, insofar as hunches in this instance just follow other hunches as opposed to hunches emerging in response to critical analysis and reflection on causation. Machinic apophenia, accordingly, can be seen as the objectified visual evidence of the power of associative thinking, teaching us to 'see', in the spirit of conspiracy theories, things and connections that lie invisibly deep within the miasma of phenomena.[82] That many of the ideologues of the technosystem

---

[80] Joanna Zylinska, ibid, pp81–82

[81] See Gottfried Leibniz, *Philosophical Papers and Letters*, edited and introduced by L.E. Loemker, Reidel, Dordrecht, 1969

[82] For a discussion of apophenia, see Benjamin Bratton, 'Some Traces of Effects of the Post-Anthropocene: On Accelerationist Geopolitical Aesthetics', *e-flux journal*, No. 46, 2013, and Hito Steyerl, 'A Sea of Data: Pattern Recognition and Corporate Animism (Forked Version)', in *Pattern Discrimination*, ibid

support this kind of pre-Kantian thinking has much to do with their self-identity as intellectual 'outriders' and their tendency to separate the tech world from the controlling interests of government bureaucracies, positing themselves as external to, or in resistance to, the structures of control they themselves put in place. Musk, Thiel, and Zuckerberg are all post-political libertarians in this sense who see governments and bureaucracies deliberately hindering their desire to rid the world of 'unnecessary mediation'. Identifying technological innovation as a positive escape from state regulation or poor competitive practice becomes, therefore, an ideology of de-governmentalization and is completely compatible with this critique of mediation. Which is why the media-tech companies are happy to facilitate or play along with conspiratorial ideologies that focus on government – and democratic accountability – as defenders of restrictive practice that inhibit market rationality and innovation. It becomes the responsibility of every citizen, according to the ideologues of post-ideology projective thinking, to search for the true hidden links between things that governments and scientific systems do not want us to see. Thus, the issue here is not 'projective thinking' as such. Abductive thinking captures how the power of associative thinking can test and probe certain given causal assumptions. But projective thinking without theory is impotent – stupid no less – and ultimately capitulates to the logic of authoritarianism: 'I know, because I know'. "The stupid are unable to make breaks or breakaways; they are hampered on a rhetorical level, for they cannot run with grammatical leaps or metonymical discontinuity. They are incapable of referring allegorically or embracing deferral,"[83] as Ronell puts it. Indeed, the machinic objectification of apophenia in its neoliberal form is evidence of what Anders calls, as I have already noted, the intellectual "self-degradation"[84] that comes from humans curtailing themselves in their attempt to "measure up to a machine". In fact, this self-degradation or

---

[83] Avital Ronell, *Stupidity*, ibid, p17
[84] Günter Anders, 'On Promethean Shame,' ibid, p49

stupidity becomes even worse when the technosystem identifies this curtailment – through apophenia – with liberty itself.

Which brings me back to O'Connell's work and the question of novelty, the gimmick, abduction, and 'system interference'. Today in the new culture wars, in which the Big Data cultural wing of the technosystem seeks to take over the so-called productive and distributive functions of the art world, the first critical priority of artists, as the very ground of abduction, the non-rational, and constitutive deficiency, is to resist the shame of humans' 'technical inability'. For it is only by resisting the shame of technical inability that constitutive deficiency and what we have been calling 'thinking stupidity' can do its system interference work – but not through technical withdrawal, as we have consistently insisted on, but through confronting technology on its own gimmick terrain. This is why O'Connell's strategies of system interference pursue a kind of counter-intrusion into the intrusiveness of the technological device or process, as if he was stalking down these technological devices and processes. Interestingly Ngai talks about the technological gimmick as that which "obtrudes",[85] the thing that sticks out to gain our attention, the thing that loudly declares its promise of efficiency, time-saving, pleasure, etc.

But the gimmick is also that which *intrudes*, its contrivances hidden by its naturalization as a discrete device, process, service, interobject, in any given system. If the device that obtrudes 'works too hard', according to Ngai, to find its consumer or paying audience, the device that intrudes is the device that hides the fact that it works hard or works efficiently at all. The need to impress has been naturalized, turned into a mute rational teleology.

So, taking into account all the functions of the technosystem and counter-artistic strategies I have mapped out so far, in order to put in place the final piece of my analysis of O'Connell's 'system interference', I would want to say that what gives a certain edge to

---

[85] Sianne Ngai, ibid, p201

the link between misuse and thinking stupidity in his art is the use of obtrusion as a kind of 'sticking out'. I'm resistant to say that obtrusion is identifiable with the gimmick per se, as if obtrusion and the gimmick were the same, because I don't believe his actions and conceptual devices are strictly gimmicks – although we might say the latest works, *#camponagolfcourse Tent* (2022), *Making Wind* (2019) and *Turbogolfing* (2019), might fit into that category. But nevertheless, I think it is fair to say that as a means of pursuing his stupefaction of computational reason, his priority, through proxies, objects and his own physical presence, is, in a sense, to *get in the way of* machines, as if in a mock 'shared dialogue' with a given digital programme or device, his principal concern is to annoy and irritate. His obtrusive actions are certainly there to gain attention – definitely – but they lay no claim to any special artistic privileges. Indeed, the obverse applies: their desire to 'stick out' becomes identifiable with the execution of simple conceptual actions or templates; there is no aesthetic inflation, no pleonastic self-advertisement, even if there is a certain formal astuteness and trickery (particularly in the new work). We can see this clearly in a relatively early piece, *Now Man*, which went through various iterations (2006–2013).

*Now Man* is crucial to understanding the later work and the refusal of O'Connell to submit to a logic of artistic making, in tandem with his commitment to a post-conceptual understanding of the tasks confronting or worthy of art today. *Now Man* consists of a hired clown (Dave Thompson, the original Tinky Winky in the BBC's *Teletubbies*) in a black suit and bowler hat, who tries to keep up with a violently swinging video camera. As O'Connell describes it: "Eventually a routine was settled upon, in which the clown would react to the movement of the swinging camera suspended from the ceiling. The LCD display screen on the camcorder was turned forward and the performer instructed to remain within frame. The performer was, in effect, tethered to the screen, which in turn was attached to the ceiling."[86] The task of the clown to stay in frame was largely impossible, given the wild and unpredictable movements of the camera; the flex to which the camera was attached would slowly wind up to the ceiling and then aggressively cascade down and whiplash out, causing the clown to dodge the camera for fear of being hit and perhaps concussed. To watch the clown try to stay in screen and dodge the violent unpredictability of the apparatus at the same time is to see, then, a simple playing out of the libidinal drama between human and machine inside the technosystem: the person is desperate to stay in screen, even if the camera makes it incredibly difficult to do so, just as the camera makes itself captivatingly evasive, forcing the person to continue, with all the risks, to stay in view of the screen. But this is not strictly a position of submission to a machine on the part of the person. The person's concern for his own safety places himself in a continuous state of instability, in which the fear of being hurt brings to consciousness the advantages of non-immersion, of not getting too close. In this sense O'Connell talks about the work as mobilizing three characters, thereby cutting across the submissive duality of human and machine: the performer (the user), the camera (the hardware), and the artist (the programmer) (himself). All are shown to have a shared, if unstable, stake in the drama. "All three have agency. Any one could be recognised as dominant or submissive and the situation is unfixed."[87] Intriguingly, O'Connell refers to Flann O'Brien's *The Third Policeman* here, and O'Brien's reflection in the novel on the perils of human-technology proximity. "Fear of close contact with things or others would appear superstitious but, maybe it has some basis. Flann O'Brien's fiction inadvertently draws attention to such anxieties. His fictional idiot/savant de Selby...may have obsessed over the significance of atoms being exchanged between bicycles and humans but psychologists and therapists frequently deal with real problems of

---

[86] Micheál O'Connell, *Art as 'Artificial Stupidity'*, PhD thesis, University of Sussex, 2016, pp56–57

[87] Micheál O'Connell, ibid, p62

attachment and transference."[88] O'Connell is not actually saying we should put humans and thinking machines together on the psychoanalyst's couch; that would be pretty much a useless Turing test type exercise. But rather, that the pertinent point raised here, which I touched on earlier in our discussion of O'Brien, is how does one build machines and to what ends, in order that humans can live and interact with machine consciousness? For O'Connell, therefore, in the here and now, there is a clear and definable artistic and cultural struggle in relation to this question: computational reason has to be *put in its place,* so to speak. Not thereby to give succour to humanists, aesthetes, eco-conservationists, and premodern nostalgists, but as the basis for radical intervention into the present interobjective and intersubjective conditions of the technosystem, as the basis for new human-machine relations. In this sense, what follows on from *Now Man,* as if the work has been a kind of founding statement of his practice, is how by embedding himself or herself in the "highly networked techno-industrial infrastructure", the artist is able to draw on "assets, artefacts, data and experience which call to be extracted and played with".[89] In this respect there is a shift in sorts from the work that descends directly from *Now Man* (*Less, Contra-Invention, Trafficking* (2020) *Immersive Interactive Installation,* (2021), and *Insecurity Camera Dance* (2021) with its direct echoes formally of *Now Man,* as O'Connell scurries around trying to stay within view of the moving surveillance camera outside of the West Cork Arts Centre) to the recent expressly Ireland themed works, *Turbogolfing* (2019), *Turbogolfing Real* (2021), *Turbine Kick* (2020), *Autofocus Feedback Loop* (2021), *Boring 2 (Drive By)* (2021), and *#camponagolfcourse Tent* and *Making Wind* (2019). For here, obtrusion as interference becomes obtrusion as a kind of calculated 'offer of help' and comic entrepreneurial endeavour as part of the international tourist industry. He creates a kind of art consultative agency with a strong resemblance to O'Brien's Research Bureau, the primary focus being Ireland's world-class golf courses. In this sense he parks his

---

[88] Micheál O'Connell, ibid, p65
[89] Micheál O'Connell, ibid, p94

obtrusive conceptual actions and devices in the public domain in a way that was not so evident in the earlier work, with its reliance on working clandestinely. He still relies on subterfuge, but here it breaks into open ground, making direct contact with those who he approaches in cheerful good faith. Thus, taking up the environmental imperative of wind farms – a common sight now in Ireland (the country has the third highest per capita power generation from wind of any nation state, mostly from onshore turbines that generate a third of Ireland's electricity) – he develops in project *Turbogolf* his version of Turbo Golf Racing (a popular arcade game involving sports cars and huge golf balls) as a possible harmonious bringing together of tourism with ecological action, that would suit all the family and expand golf's appeal: golf wind farms that double as giant crazy golf courses – celebrations of energy efficiency, industrial architecture and the Irish comedic spirit. To pursue this aim over the past few years, O'Connell has posted various 'Turbo Golf' reviews on Tripadvisor for golf courses and resorts in Ireland and around the world (appropriately Google translated), accompanied by rudimentary if nonetheless convincing mock-ups of his imaginary courses. Trump International Golf Club in Dubai wrote back in Arabic thanking O'Connell for his visit and inviting him to come again soon. Many, however, did not and Tripadvisor took the mock-ups down immediately. The tactical subversion of the early work here becomes a slightly demented over-identification with the neoliberal entrepreneurial spirit of the 'new consumer experience': why can't golf be reinvented and subject to the law of the gimmick? Why can't golf find a new demographic that integrates what is technically advanced and woke about Irish energy policy into a new popular culture? Why can't the best of Ireland (the beauty of the well-husbanded sward) and the beauty of Irish invention and engineering (the virile and sleek wind turbine) find a common home? O'Brien would have certainly loved O'Connell's cheek; but I think he would have singled out for particular commendation the work's delirious, monumental demoticism: the transformation of well-apportioned discreteness and landscaped charm into an uglified technological sublime, inverting the anti-sumptuary logic of the best luxury golf experiences into a family playground that combines the pleasures of both eco-friendly industry and rustic views. If his plan has an air of neoliberal rationality and conceivability about it – 'why shouldn't golf get a makeover; golf is dismally underthought' – nonetheless it also embraces a revolutionary and Jacobin 'levelling' that pushes obtrusion into outright occupancy and appropriation. His *Turbogolf* courses sweep through partitions, borders, boundaries, enclaves, in a kind of a Promethean reordering of the tightly coiled spaces of Irishness. In this I am reminded of the kindred provocation of Eimear Walshe's video *The Land Question* (2020), in which Walshe incites a public campaign for outdoor sex in the Irish countryside in order to unravel an Irish colonial narrative of enclosure, expropriation and confinement. But if in *Turbogolf* the physical restructuring of the landscape has the detached air of fantasy, in O'Connell's next work, *#camponagolfcourse Tent,* the disruptive occupancy of the golf course as a sylvan dream space has a more direct, even immediately threatening reality: the collaging of tents on promotion shots of the Old Head Golf Links in Kinsale, County Cork. The parking of tents on the Old Head course on Twitter and Instagram looked like a convincing call for campers or the tented homeless and golf clubs to find some common cause. Indeed, so striking did the hacked promotion shots look that it appeared that this was part of a new kind of advocacy: golf, the home of a gentle, well-tended, and restful social justice. This humour might seem like a step back from the earlier uses of obtrusion. Here the deflation of computational reason takes the more conventional form of public image inversion, and indeed, contrary to what I've argued above, image *production* as opposed to image negation, or the anti-aesthetic tracking of the vacuity of the technical image inside the vast networks of image detritus that compose the surveillance functions of the technosystem, as reflected in *Less* and other earlier works. These new images are composed, prepped. This means, in turn, that the conceptual gimmick is very much out in the open, so to speak, a purposeful visual disruption of the continuum of certain social and cultural expectations that, in fact, reveal no shame about 'trying too hard'. Indeed, to achieve this perverse optimism O'Connell calls on the overweening social-design mentality of the futurist Blue Sky PowerPoint. The images face off the future with confidence; this is where 'thinking upstream' takes you, they implore. Thus, even though O'Connell self-consciously adopts the obtrusive gimmick as a means of over-identification with the neoliberal entrepreneurial vision (inviting stupidity to the party) strangely the Turbo Golf interventions do not appear cynical despite their disruptive logic. This is because their super-animated and absurd Jacobin futurism appears under current economic and cultural conditions – Free golf from its timid, aging constraints! - weirdly 'neoliberal reasonable.' This leaves the reception of Turbo Golf at the mercy of the perverse pleasure or *jouissance* of the projected rationality of technical innovation and novelty, as demonstrated so vividly in na Gopaleen's ice melter of the snows of yesteryear – 'in no sense is this useful, helpful, but nevertheless I can see the point of it'. Which is also, we might say, not an unreasonable working definition of desire and of art: 'now I see that this exists, I can see it should exist'. But O'Connell in the *Turbogolf* works is not at one artistically with this vision; although the obtrusiveness of the wind turbine golf course imaginatively captures a would-be eco-sensitive neoliberal future for our inspection it is not a vision that he wants to realize in material form. This is because these aggressive comedic interventions into the language of social design and social space and the modern Irish (colonial) imaginary, skirt close to the thing O'Connell doesn't want to hear as a post-conceptual artist: 'yes, I can see what you're doing let's talk about it, I can see this working'. If capital and patrons were to come calling, he has no desire to see his visions realized as actual constructions, even as a one-off alternative theme park or as an elephantine art installation. O'Connell's relationship with his materials and knowledge is quite different therefore – despite all favourable comparisons – with O'Brien's busy, helpful inventions and local, small-scale constructivist ethos. Hence the constellation of various golf and wind turbine objects in the exhibition at Uillinn is a way of offsetting this comforting approach to constructivism; in contrast to the 'uplift' of the digital images, the objects hang about as bathetic fragments, warning signs about artists inflating their role and critical potential, the remnant evidence of what I have pointed to as his "discomfort with 'making'". [90] So: there are real world limits to O'Connell's gimmick's digital cod-Wagnerian obtrusion, certainly for an artist like himself who has no interest in adding more objects to the world. The mock-ups should stay as mock-ups, stay in the realm of the mockingly innovative; and the presentation of objects should look indifferent to their possible usefulness; anything else is monstrous.

In these terms, O'Connell's fundamental resistance to his own phantasmatic vision in these later works gives us further pause for thought about the artist's relationship to his materials and knowledge under the constructivist technosystem paradigm. O'Connell blocks off or suspends two temptations for artists: the temptation to *become* a machine and the temptation to participate as an artist-technician in a Promethean reconstructivist vision of the capitalist technosystem, in which, as I mentioned earlier, the artist's technical concerns are directed to building new things, or tracking the complexities of the interobjective, technological landscape. O'Connell certainly uses machines and submits himself to their computational logic. He also takes the critical understanding, tracking and possession of the interobjective processes of the technosystem seriously. But at the same time, he realizes that without misusing machines the first position leads to passivity and machine aestheticism, and without resistance to the knowledge fetishism of the second position – the would-be complete cognitive mastery of the system – research leads to a kind of impotent delirium, in which there is no end to the mapping process. The artist becomes as subordinate to the computational logic of the technosystem as the machine-artist does to the banal preset algorithms of the fatuous AI painter machine. There is something of this knowledge delirium in Trevor Paglen's work, for instance, whose massive critical investment in understanding and locating the secret military networks of technological research and

---

[90] Micheál O'Connell, *Art as 'Artificial Stupidity'*, ibid, p44

their place in the technosystem leads less to usable and stable knowledge than to a feeling of endless incompletion, data overkill and subjective indifference. This is the same sense of impotence, paradoxically, that has faced the casual users of the Wikileaks files (one needs teams of researchers and powerful search engines to get anything out of the material, meaning that one of the striking advantages of the vast scale of Big Data is that it can hide in plain sight). As Alberto Toscano and Jeff Kinkle admit, in a relatively supportive defence of this form of post-Critical Art Ensemble 'system interference' art, inside these networks the links between the economy, state, military, and technosystem become forbiddingly unmappable for the lone artist or artists, and inevitably leads the failure of knowledge into the comforting pathways of conspiracy theory and speculative associative thinking, the things that this kind of cognitive mapping set out to challenge in the first place. "An inability cogently to map or understand the complexities of global capitalism is supplemented by paranoid visions of nefarious elites and cabals bent on world domination. The panorama generated by conspiracy theory appears to fall into the traps of the hubristic attempt to 'see it whole'..."[91] Indeed these feelings of impotence in the face of the technological sublime by the lone researcher or group of researchers easily leads the artist into the domain of the visionary or obsessive artist-technician driven by the pursuit of the telling detail that never ends. This is not to say, given these limitations, that artists are therefore forced to submit to the opacity of the technosystem and pursue the aesthetic option, thereby avoiding intensive research work in their art. But that 'knowledge fetishism', as it transforms into system representation and system building, can easily diminish the political efficacy of the work's reception and legibility, because in the very act of cognitive mapping, the complexities and opacities of the research are passed undigested onto the viewer and reader. Unless, that is, the complexity of the mapping is radically detextualized and reduced to a sequence of

---

[91] Alberto Toscano and Jeff Kinkle, *Cartographies of the Absolute*, Zer0 Books, John Hunt Publishing, Alresford, Hants, 2014, p69

aesthetic signs, as in Paglen's photo archives, which seek to anchor the hidden research in the visual orientation of the photo-documentary sequence. But strangely, in finding a visual correlative the specificities of the research are dissolved. The call to a new and intensive cognitive mapping ends up as a series of enigmatic visual encounters with the dark, off-map geographies of the digital surveillance state, producing a naturalized visual continuum between the outward appearances of the interobject world of surveillance technologies and the power of state and technosystem.[92] In this sense, confronted by the need to produce images defined by the reach and intrusiveness of the technological sublime, the artist, tends, on this basis, to inadvertently produce a vision of technological inevitabilism.

O'Connell, takes another pathway by refusing 'knowledge fetishism', or rather refuses to put the artist in the position of 'knowledge provider'. For not only does this delimit what art is particularly good at – the critical disinvestment of knowledge from the neutral claims of 'enlightenment' – but also weakens the exposure of capitalist reason through the denaturalization of form and process. This is why technological and technical misuse, 'thinking stupidity', abduction and the non-rational have played such an important part in my account of art and the technosystem so far. For they all disinvest knowledge – today the power of computational reason – from unexamined assumptions about progress and enlightenment under computational logic. Indeed, both the critical denaturalization of the link between knowledge and 'enlightenment' and the misuse of the processes of capitalist reason are tightly connected here in my reading of O'Connell's art. But if this shines some light between the artist as technical provider

---

[92] See Trevor Paglen, *Blank Spots on the Map: The Dark Geography of the Pentagon's Secret World*, Dutton, Penguin Group, New York, 2009

and the artist as technical misuser, we are still faced with a deep crisis of art and the artist as it confronts the derationalizing and nihilistic interests of the technosystem that underwrite the posthuman mandate.

The constructivist position, which I would include O'Connell in, despite my criticism of the position here, remains politically weak given the severe constraints on popular participation in the remaking of the technical system. This demonstrates the first law of capital: the accumulation of capital is not simply about wealth creation, but the power to determine investment decisions and the limits of the free action of the majority outside of waged labour; that is, the power to narrow free action not determined by market choices. As Utsa Patnaik and Prabhat Patnaik have put this in their analysis of neoliberalism and imperialism, what is at stake in capital maintaining its control of investment is always the *social power* of capital, its room for financial manoeuvre against government fiscal authority and popular action. This is the reason why finance capital remains so opposed to state debt and is obsessed with 'balancing the books'. For if governments can increase investment and increase employment through public works (and even sustain profits for capital) macroeconomic activity encroaches on capitalists' decision-making powers. The thing finance capital fears most, consequently, if governments of the left do manage to increase state debt in defiance of cuts in public spending, is that governments which follow "may widen state intervention even further" at the cost of capitalists' decision-making powers. [93] Finance capital, therefore, produces an 'epistemic closure' around financial responsibility as a claim on capitalists' greater stewardship of the economy, which has a huge ideological impact on the power of capitalist economic agency to define social reproduction from the position of 'individual

---

[93] Utsa Patnaik and Prabhat Patnaik, *Capital and Imperialism: Theory, History, and the Present*, Monthly Review Press, New York, 2021, p198

responsibility'. [94] This has been particularly the case under neoliberalism, where the state, far from backing state intervention in the interests of its own populations, now intervenes on behalf of the interests of global capital or on behalf of those private interests that intersect with local national interests. Thus, one of the far-reaching consequences of privatization has been the internalization of financial structures and the increasing incorporation of non-financial enterprises into financial processes – international finance stripping out profits from national public resources. Under neoliberal privatization, public services and forms of social provision have been opened up to 'debt rationalization' as a way of delinking value from public goods. As Costas Lapavitsas notes, "individuals and households have come increasingly to rely on the formal financial system to facilitate access to vital goods and services, including housing, education, health and transport".[95]

The hegemony of the modern technosystem therefore both serves and is shaped by this epistemic closure, this stripping out of the commons. We see this most obviously with the commercial transformation of the internet. In order, for something as powerful as the internet to remain under the control of capital and commercial exchange it had to be financialized in ways that prevented the network from remaining an open source. But to destroy it as an open source would destroy its functionality and centrality to digital capitalism's ideology of global communication and the free passage of goods. As Feenberg puts it: "Embedding a strict regime of intellectual property in the technology of the

---

[94] For a discussion of the US dollar-power of this control, see Marco D'Eramo, 'American Decline?', *New Left Review*, No. 135, May/June 2022. "What the US controls – through the dollar system and, not unrelatedly, the scale of its financial markets – are the mechanisms that regulate, advance, obstruct and in some cases (blocking SWIFT access) even paralyse the flow of capital." (p13)
[95] Costas Lapavitsas, *Profiting Without Producing: How Finance Exploits Us All*, Verso, London and New York, 2013, p4

system would be incompatible with free communicative action."[96] It had to be financialized, then, in such a way as to make participation under conditions of epistemic closure a pleasurable and involving experience that allowed users to think of it, and participate in it, as a free 'community' of users. Thus, the big commercial social media providers have avoided paywalls, generating revenue through bringing users and advertisers into a kind of personalized cohabitation, enabling users' interests and desires to be modified through modes of attention that reward online participation and providing the pleasurable reinforcement of homophily. Hence the success of the internet lies in the fact that it is not simply an instrumental electronic exposure *to* markets; on the contrary, it mobilizes desires and interests as part of a free community, indeed global community of users. Feenberg sees the internet sanguinely, therefore, as capital adopting the interests of commerce to community, and thereby takes the internet to be a contested space between the 'consumption model' and the 'community model'. There is some truth in the notion that the internet remains a communal space driven by those who use it. However, definitions of use remain naïve if free participation at the point of access is identifiable with user autonomy, particularly when we look at the internet's fundamental place in neoliberalism's massive refunctioning of capital's epistemic closure around the inviolability of the market. This is because the internet's central place in the technosystem revolves around the production and facilitation of consumers' and users' adaptation to what I called earlier the aesthetic functions of mature capitalism, and what I identify here more precisely as the intersection between the libidinal economy of mature capitalism and the libidinal economy of the capitalist subject. In these terms there is no 'contested space' on the internet between a 'consumption model' and a 'community model' but, rather, the production of a 'community model' for 'individuated' ends. Indeed, free access is defined by a powerful attachment to a model of communication in which pleasure and the pursuit of individuation is driven and

---

[96] Andrew Feenberg, *Technosystem: The Social Life of Reason*, ibid, p106

shaped by the internalization of, and addiction to, the smoothly efficient and multiplicitous sensuous interspaces of computational reason's automation of information and human interaction. The experience of community, in these terms, *is* the experience of 'individuation'. Through the integration of the visual, text and sound, as James Bridle declares, computation "does not merely augment, frame, and shape culture; by operating beneath our everyday, casual awareness of it, it actually *becomes* culture".[97] In other words, the internet's employment of computational reason towards socially inclusive and homophilic ends is the means by which digital or platform capitalism adapts democracy to the epistemic closure of market rationality. But if the outcome is coercive, the methods are not. As Bernard Stiegler outlines in his major critique of contemporary libidinal economy,[98] the internet enables a massive reordering and rechannelling of attention and self-affection in the interests of what he calls the exteriorized proletarianization of knowledge and creativity of the many, proletarianization being that which excludes workers and citizens from the production and knowledge of things beyond their own immediate competences and concerns. Proletarianization "presupposes the liquidation of both *savoir-faire* [knowledge of how to make or do] and *savoir-vivre* [knowledge of how to live]".[99] But for Stiegler, in an echo of Günther Anders, this is not perceived overall by users as a loss. On the contrary, the libidinal economy under the sway of computational reason organizes desires through opposing the efficiency of (machinic) pleasure – the immediate mediated pleasure taken in things and bodies – to that of the *inefficiency*, even impotence, of an enfeebled noesis and otium (the

---

[97] James Bridle, *New Dark Age: Technology and the End of the Future*, Verso, London and New York, 2018, p39

[98] See in particular Bernard Stiegler, *The Neganthropocene*, Open Humanities Press, London, 2018, and *The Age of Disruption: Technology and Madness in Computational Capitalism*, Polity Press, Cambridge, 2019

[99] Bernard Stiegler, *For a New Critique of Political Economy*, Polity Press, Cambridge, 2010, p16

ancient Roman term for the time of self-reflection and studious leisure). "The time of the passage to the noetic act [the rational, creative act] is that of *otium*, which does not at all mean idle time, yet does mean the time of leisure, that is, of freedom and of 'care of the self'."[100] The question of epistemic closure in these terms, consequently, is defined through the heightened identification of pleasure with the encouragement of self-loss and the diminishment of humans as reading and interpreting bodies; for the reflective and interpreting body is too tied to the extended temporalities of noesis and otium and its negative capacity for disruption and delay, to stabilize the subject's pleasurable and efficient market immersion. The production of knowledge always threatens to produce critique and an inefficient distance between thought and action. This is why the primary function of capital's epistemic closure is to dissolve those processes and sites of 'unmanageable knowledge' or subaltern knowledge that would disrupt, slow down, or derail the accumulation process. The libidinal economy's production of pleasure, in its struggle against noesis and otium, derives from what appears as the greater rewards that come with the loss of self. There is, accordingly, no need for the market to explicitly rationalize these guarantees, for the 'reason of pleasure' (the release of the subject from the would-be 'unpleasure' of noesis and otium) is freely able to do its ideological work without ideological exhortation; if the available pleasure gives pleasure – sustained pleasure – the loss of self is no great loss, given that it relieves some of the pain and disappointment of the 'thinking [noetic] self'. Thus, the reliance on computational reason is mobilized precisely through identifying the greater efficacy of pleasure with the time of immediate rewards, as opposed to long term self-determined desires. For Stiegler this not only weakens the place of the noetic and otium in the lives of the majority, it also increases the submission of democratic politics and governance to the overwhelming imperatives of market rationality. "When disenchantment becomes absolute, the power of the powerful plays out *without*

---

[100] Bernard Stiegler, ibid, pp53–54

*consistence,* without relation to *otium* of any kind, without the slightest belief, and therefore as absolute *cynicism*: with neither faith nor law," [101] producing an economy and culture of fundamental "carelessness".[102]

Under these conditions the issue of apophenia, therefore, passes over to something more threatening inside the libidinal economy of the technosystem; that is, the way that these pleasures of least resistance lead to cultural and social *impotentiality* – the notion that capitalism in its mature phase, despite its powerful eudaemonic emphasis on self-realization, is structurally and psychologically disposed to weaken the actualization of human potentiality. This understanding is the very opposite of the positive account of failure in Žižek's reading of non-potentiality. Whereas Žižek defends failure from a position of negation in the struggle with and transformation of computational reason – that human value is not a condition of being measured against the machinic – the impotentiality that proceeds from apophenia and technological shame leads directly to the incorporation of humans into the technosystem and into the realm of completed nihilism. There is thus a counter-intuitive notion contained here. Machines do not simply take over human potentiality and 'defeat' it, rather they expose what humans already know and repeatedly have forgotten under modernity: that humanity is not capable of competing with the machinic, and therefore the loss of human potentiality is nothing to mourn. In other words, humans can legitimately extinguish their autonomy and exceptionalism in front of technology – through the pleasure- technological adaptation – because technology has exposed the fact that *there is no* core set of human powers *to potentialize,* no human powers worth developing and comparing to those provided by machines now or in the future. As Clare Colebrook says in *Death of the PostHuman* (2014), "our humanity is not an actuality from which we can draw grounds for action. The fact that we forget our *impotentiality* – that

---

[101] Bernard Stiegler, ibid, p63
[102] Bernard Stiegler, ibid, p126

we treat humans as factual beings with a normality that dictates action – has reached crisis point in modernity, especially as we increasingly suspend the *thought* of our fragility for the sake of ongoing efficiency."[103] There is a structural failure to actualize those resources and capacities that would distinguish our humanness.

Consequently, impotentiality is not an ideology of self-sabotage, but a recognition that humans' intellectual and creative capacity to produce other machines – more powerful machines – means, in reality, that human potentiality is the potentiality of machines and not the potentiality of humans. In this, impotentiality is the ideological separation of humans from machines in the name of humans' rational submission to technology and the transition of human morphology and consciousness into the machinic and posthuman. But there is a fundamental aporia to this nihilistically rational teleology. In order for machines to be engineered like humans, machine-humans have at some point to *live like* humans, as humans, in order to generate and store the necessary reflective, contextual, semantic, emotive, and abductive knowledge to act in ways that link consciousness to practice and labour. But to be able to do this these machines have to know insufficiency, conflict, doubt, error, loss, and failure as a condition of thinking and acting. This means that there is no posthuman exit from constitutive deficiency, unless that is the posthuman human-machine is designated as not strictly human, but human-like. Because if human-machines become as insufficient, uncertain, and delimited in their thinking and action as humans, then there seems little value in the advocacy of the posthuman as the radical supersession and incorporation of the human into the supra-posthuman. The morphological immortality of these human-like posthumans may be no guarantee of post-biological success either. Human-like humans may want to live the life span of humans, as a condition of solidarity with their human counterparts, unless they are willing

[103] Claire Colebrook, *Death of the PostHuman: Essays on Extinction, Vol. 1*, Open Humanities Press, London, 2014, p13

to become the non-human ambassadors and agents of space exploration and the colonization of Mars and further. For as we know, biological humans cannot *live* in space. Space is continuously washed by intense waves of radiation and rapidly moving particles, destroying the chemical bonds of cells; any living body that is exposed to the vacuum of space would inflate and rupture immediately; under weightlessness muscles lose mass, bones lose calcium, and red blood cell levels decline; there is no air resistance in space, the orbital velocity of Earth is five miles a second, and objects retain this velocity indefinitely (until that is they collide with another object and produce many more whizzing objects); and because of these extreme conditions primary materials are yet to be industrially processed beyond the Earth's atmosphere.[104] The posthuman project, accordingly, may in fact radically bifurcate the human and the machinic, rather than reintegrate them into the would-be singularity, leaving, on the one hand, humans, still tied to sexual reproduction, agriculture, habitation, and painful finitude; and on the other hand, human-like humans, employed for their extraordinary computational skills across a vast range of disciplines and practices, and engineered for space travel and exploration, but nevertheless desperate to have their computational power reduced to a level in which intelligence and stupidity can find some common ground; indeed, having reached this threshold of technological divergence from the human, human-like humans may out of necessity have learned to love and make mistakes.[105]

---

[104] For a brilliant assessment of the technosystem on a global and cosmological scale, and a critique of the unthought posthumanism of the new Prometheans (Elon Musk et al.) and space expansionism, see Daniel Deudney, *Dark Skies: Space Expansionism, Planetary Geopolitics, and the Ends of Humanity*, Oxford University Press, Oxford, 2020

[105] For a tender though radically unsentimental fictive account of the non-human learning from the contingent pleasures, sadness and disappointments of humanness, see Olga Ravn's novel set on a 22nd century spaceship run by humanoids and humans, in which the human employees are eventually eliminated by the company, as the

## Conclusion: Laughter and Persistence

Where do these final reflections leave us then? Where have we arrived with this speculative sci-fi scenario? Where do the very real coercive conditions of the technosystem and libidinal economy leave art and the artist in the wider sense? What kind of technological scales can the artist expect to work under in the near future? And how does O'Connell's model of 'system interference', indeed, square up to the forbidding extensity of human incorporation into what is now a machinic civilization? I ask this last question in all seriousness even if, in an important way, it is the wrong question. For as I have tried to show, one of the remaining critical functions of the artist in this machinic civilization is for the artist to act contingently on those materials, signs, processes, devices, and gimmicks that can reveal where domination and instrumental values do their deliberative work; artists then should not feel that they need to speak on behalf of the future of humanity in the abstract, when they can demonstrate a range of cognitive and practical skills that show art's transformative potential as a common and shared resource. This expresses what I have discussed as social constructivism's alternative rationalization of technological development. But should artists today in the spirit of the 1920s be technicians? I like the idea of artists as technicians. I like the fact that artists know

---

humanoids begin to think beyond their computationally preset function as labourers: *The Employees: A workplace novel of the 22nd century*, Lolli Editions, London, 2020. "I know without a doubt that I'm real. I may have been made, but now I'm making myself." (p87). The point, here, then, is for the posthuman to function as a new making of the human, the computational delinking of the posthuman from the human will make this task narrow and self-thwarting, in the end excluding the posthuman from the meaning of the human; posthumans may look like humans, may even superficially sound like humans, but they won't be humans or possess key human attributes.

stuff and can do stuff in relation to the interobjective technological world they choose to inhabit. It means that artists see no distinction between action, knowledge, and creativity. But is the relationship between action, knowledge, and creativity enough? Can it see the artist through those forces that would capture these good intentions in the name of social engagement, when social engagement is never far from the interests of capital and abstract labour? I argue this not because art's social claims are always compromised – which is to say nothing, as the business of engagement is to know it is compromised – but because artists have other things to do rather than bring 'knowledge to communities' or trying to ameliorate ills. Artists cannot therefore simply adopt the use-values of a dominant functionality, for this dominant functionality is always crossed and bisected by dominant power relations that would reduce the options of the artist to that of democracy's 'little helper'. This is why there is a fundamental difference between artist-*as*-technicians and artists *becoming* technicians, hiring themselves out on social projects, that encourages artists to think of themselves as involved in expanding the 'usefulness' of art. This 'usefulness' if it turns out to be useful, is mainly useful for the assimilation of art into the neoliberal ideal of artists as service providers; so perhaps being useful has to be something else, something very different from being a 'little helper'. To work *as* a technician, accordingly, is not to confuse the artist's pursuit of knowledge simply with the social application of that knowledge; it is to open, rather, a critical relationship to knowledge and power as a means of bringing the critique of knowledge to bear on capitalist relations. And today, as we have seen, the dominant relationship between knowledge and capitalist relations is predicated on an overwhelming set of assumptions about the efficiency and functional and cultural privileges of computational reason. The challenge to digital capitalism, therefore, cannot be based methodologically, solely on adjusting the narrow and restrictive coding patterns of algorithms, of shifting the crude parameters of 'behavioural modification', as if computational reason under capitalist conditions can 'stabilize' itself as a neutral provider of information and human interaction;

computational reason under capitalist conditions *is* 'behavioural modification' – *all the way down*. And, consequently, we can see why aspects of the constructivist model of popular participation and the refunctioning of the technosystem fit comfortably into the liberal call for a more 'friendly business model', for the idea of privileging of algorithmic change serves to reinforce the idea that epistemic closure is nothing more than a technical problem and that art's 'usefulness' is best served by following this.

So, the artist's role in the critique of technology under capitalism, if it is to offer more than sanguine adjustment to the technical base of the technosystem, or humanist homilies about avoiding 'manipulation', must push the declared rationality of computational reason into a state of bathos. Indeed, so powerful is the self-rationalizing enchantment of machines, to not do so is to assume that the answer to human-machine relations must always be on technology's terms, as if technology has no masters. And this is the reason why the misuse of materials and processes in art as outlined here is so crucial to this critique and what we might call a 'counter-engineering' of the technosystem, in the spirit of early modernism and the avant-garde. For misuse does not mean a critique of technology as such, but an insistence on the defunctioning or refunctioning of technical processes and technological devices as a denaturalization of technology as 'natural evolution'. By such defunctioning and refunctioning the interobjective and intersubjective relations of the technosystem are shown to be contingent, the outcome of human practice and labour, and thus dependent on extra-technological decisions and values. The would-be impotentiality of the human condition, therefore, is a cunning and expedient ideology, given that in reality it is based on mature capitalism's "intrinsic disposability"[106] of people and things and not on the fateful evidence of humans' final and inevitable overcoming of themselves through technological evolution. The misuse of technology, presently, then, has nothing to lose in setting itself up as a practice of 'thinking stupidity', for

---

[106] Bernard Stiegler, *For a New Critique of Political Economy*, ibid, p86

the critique of technological evolution cannot be won by rational counter-proposals alone; critique also has to make technological evolution functionally *senseless and grotesque*. And O'Connell, understands this better than most, as a condition of finding a workable subjective place for the artist both inside and outside of the technosystem. For to be 'stupid', to comically deflate or overinvest in the good faith of computational reason, is to arrest technology's implacability, its foundational self-importance, enabling a subjective disjointedness to enter the picture, a reassertion of the creativeness of insufficiency. O'Connell's link between defunctionality and the comedy of misapplication thus serves not to simply disenchant our experience of technology – for we are no longer in the kind of world that mourns the pre-technological and the pre-modern as a source of restitutive humanity. As Yuk Hui says: "Our engagement with technical systems is no longer the same as the encounter between *Dasein* and simple tools such as the telescope. Inside the system or an ensemble, decisions are systematically determined by algorithms instead of relying on the subjective selection of significations."[107] But rather, defunctionality and misapplication opens a space where practice and thinking can disorient the teleological and calculable as a means of generating "new techniques of orientation", [108] new relationships between knowledge, technology, and pleasure. Misuse and comedic disruption consequently provide a gap, a caesura, *through* which the transformation of insufficiency (abduction) and the pursuit of the non-rational can pass. And this importantly is why the comedic is not to be confused here with one of comedy's more conventional functions, indeed one of its mainstream functions: as consolation for our finitude, namely the idea that the uplift of comedy, in situations of dire constraint or overreaching hubris after our ideals have soured, enables us to reconnect with our weaknesses and imperfections as a species ('we're only human after all'), which is our contemporary (anti) grand narrative. Laughter in these terms

---

[107] Yuk Hui, *On the Existence of Digital Objects*, ibid, p223
[108] Yuk Hui, *Art and Cosmotechnics*, ibid, p275

'settles us', for it reconnects us to our reassuring 'smallness'. And this is why the redemptive function of comedy can just as easily perpetrate the constraints and oppression of a situation by making repression and oppression bearable. But if comedy questions the temptations of unguarded transcendentalism it also uses these limits to desert the internal limits of finitude itself, the fact that finitude is always a "failed finitude",[109] as Alenka Zupančič argues in *The Odd One In: On Comedy* (2008); that is, a point of inflexion and splitting, in which humans reject and deny their finitude as a refusal of mere humanness. Comedy thereby is not simply the reason of limits submerging itself into mundane materiality as a condition of cutting humanity down to size, it takes the laughter generated by insufficiency, failure, and loss to be a moment of reflection, where miscalculation, misunderstanding and mistakes release humans from their mute materiality, their reconciliation with their 'tragic' constraints. "Is not the very existence of comedy and of the comical telling us most clearly that a man is never just a man, and that his finitude is very much corroded by a passion which is precisely not cut to the measure of man and his finitude...the flaws, extravagances, excesses, and so-called human weaknesses of comic characters are precisely what account for their *not* being 'only human'. More precisely, they show us that what is 'human' exists only in this kind of excess over itself."[110] Comedy, therefore, is not just a space where we are allowed to happily feel attached to our finitude, but also a moment of excess through our acceptance of failure and miscalculation, a potentially "surplus, empty place of subjectivity that constitutes the playground of any possible change".[111]

O'Connell's comedic understanding of art and the technosystem is anti-Bergsonian in this respect, insofar as by opening up a space for new techniques of orientation he doesn't place comedy or the

---

[109] Alenka Zupančič, *The Odd One In: On Comedy*, MIT Press, Cambridge Mass. and London, 2008, p52
[110] Alenka Zupančič, ibid, p49
[111] Alenka Zupančič, Ibid, p217

comedic effect on the side of *life,* against technology and automation. The functions of technology and automation are not extraneous, denaturalizing, and destructive of the human, as Hui touches on above, but the material infrastructure through which subjectivity and spirit *find their bearings*; and therefore, insofar as we are able to claim the history of the human as identifiable with the technical emergence of human capacity and skill through the development of the *technē*-technological relations, the human and extra-human under these conditions are indivisible, the interconnected ground of how humans make sense of the world and act in it. Comedy in the technosystem for O'Connell, then, has two specific roles to play: firstly, more obviously, the employment of satire, mockery, the sardonic, and deflation, as a means of opening power and appearances up to the destabilizing force of denaturalization; and secondly the capacity of comedy through its subjective excess to overcome the internalization of humans' happy reconciliation with shame in front of machines and human impotentiality and their shared stupidity. And this is why unlike tragedy, which submits to the past, comedy's excess lies precisely in its logic of futural persistence: its refusal to accept that failure and miscalculation determine the future on the basis of the failure of futures past. But this is not the persistence that conceives of a return to do again what has been done to do it 'better', but to do again in the name of what has been done differently and continue to do it differently, even as it fails again, as it surely will. This involves, in Hegelian terms, a drama of misrecognition, a ceaseless comedy of revision and mistakes, in which our aims and outcome are always mismatched, generating another revised aim and mismatched outcome.[112] The comedic resides, consequently, not just in our capacity to 'make strange' through an idiotic acting out or confrontation with stupidity (which as Ronell notes takes all forms, rational and irrational) but also in the fact that practice and thought are *in themselves comedic,* in as much as the exit from finitude and the restless comedy of absolute spirit never ends, and

---

[112] See Gillian Rose, *Mourning Becomes the Law: Philosophy and Representation,* Cambridge University Press, Cambridge, 1996, p71

because it never ends it has to recognize that learning to fail again is a liberation *and* an endless 'training' towards a goal that never finishes. But if comedy enables us to escape a tragic or banal finitude, this persistence – the persistence of failing, allowing us to fail freely again – does not mean that comedy's excess is free of stupidity itself. If comedy is not the redemptive force that brings us *back to life* (from an alienated technological realm that forecloses on life), neither is it the strategic and heroic key to the transformative constructive work of 'system interference'. The spirit of comedy may persist against the odds in the face of an inert materiality, and create a pathway for emancipatory reason, but we should not confuse it with reason itself. At some point we do have to stop laughing and start building, even if we can have a good old laugh at what we've built, before we start building again. Thus, in the current period, as O'Connell acknowledges in his body of relentless digressions, aporias, and grotesque repetitions, the stand-up comedian and the comedic-artist are themselves no strangers to unthinking stupidity, for the temptation is to think that comedy has the last laugh, when in fact what it offers, albeit with all persistence, are moments of respite.

## Bibliography

Adorno, Theodor, and Horkheimer, Max, *Dialectic of Enlightenment* [1947], translated by John Cumming, Verso, London and New York, 2016

Anders, Günther, 'On Promethean Shame', in *Prometheanism: Technology, Digital Culture and Human Obsolescence*, ed. Christopher John Müller, Rowman & Littlefield International, London and New York, 2016

Anders, Günther, *Die Antiquiertheit des Menschen 1: Über die Seelle im Zeitalter der zweiten industriellen Revolution* [1956], C.H.Beck, Munich, 2002

Arvatov, Boris, *Art and Production*, eds. John Roberts and Alexei Penzin, with an introduction by John Roberts and an afterword by Alexei Penzin, translated by Shushan Avagyan, Pluto Press, London, 2017

Beech, Amanda, Mackay, Robin, and Wiltgen, James, eds. *Construction Site for Possible Worlds*, Urbanomic, Falmouth, 2020

Bergson, Henri, *Laughter: An Essay on the Meaning of the Comic* [1911], translated by Cloudesley Brereton and Fred Rothwell, Green Integer, Copenhagen and Los Angeles, 1999

Bernes, Jasper, *The Work of Art in the Age of Deindustrialization*, Stanford University Press, Stanford, 2017

Böhme, Gernot, *Critique of Aesthetic Capitalism*, translated by Edmund Jephcott, Mimesis International, Italy, 2017

Bratton, Benjamin, 'Some Traces of Effects of the Post-Anthropocene: On Accelerationist Geopolitical Aesthetics', *e-flux journal*, No. 46, 2013

Bridle, James, *New Dark Age: Technology and the End of the Future*, Verso, London and New York, 2018

Burnham, Jack, *Beyond Modern Sculpture: The Effects of Science and Technology on the Sculpture of This Century*, George Braziller, New York, 1968

Chun, Wendy Hui Kyong, 'Queerying Homophily', in Clemens Apprich, Wendy Hui Kyong Chun, Florian Cramer, and Hito

Steyerl, *Pattern Discrimination,* meson press, Lüneberg, and University of Minnesota Press, Minneapolis 2018

Colebrook, Claire, *Death of the PostHuman: Essays on Extinction, Vol. 1,* Open Humanities Press, London, 2014

Critical Art Ensemble, *The Electronic Disturbance,* Autonomedia, Brooklyn, New York, 1994

D'Eramo, Marco, 'American Decline?', *New Left Review,* No. 135, May/June 2022

De Sousa Santos, Boaventura, *Epistemologies of the South: Justice Against Epistemicide,* Routledge, Abingdon, 2014

Deudney, Daniel, *Dark Skies: Space Expansionism, Planetary Geopolitics, and the Ends of Humanity,* Oxford University Press, Oxford, 2020

Donaldson, William [Henry Root], *The Henry Root Letters,* Sphere, London, 1981

Fallada, Hans, *Little Man – What Now*? [1932], translated by Susan Bennett, afterword by Philip Brady, Melville House, New York, 2009

Feenberg, Andrew, *Technosystem: The Social Life of Reason,* Harvard University Press, Cambridge Mass. and London, 2017

Hegel, G.W.F., *Phenomenology of Spirit* [1807], translated by A.V. Miller with an analysis of the text and foreword by J.N. Findlay, Oxford University Press, Oxford, 1979

Hui, Yuk, *On the Existence of Digital Objects,* foreword by Bernard Stiegler, University of Minnesota Press, Minneapolis and London, 2016

Hui, Yuk, *Art and Cosmotechnics,* e-flux/University of Minnesota Press, Minneapolis, 2021

Kafka, Franz, *The Trial* [1925], translated by Idris Parry, Penguin Classics, London, 2019

Lanier, Jaron, *Ten Arguments for Deleting Your Social Media Accounts Right Now,* Vintage, Penguin Books, London, 2018

Lapavitsas, Costas, *Profiting Without Producing: How Finance Exploits Us All,* Verso, London and New York, 2013

Larson, Erick J., *The Myth of Artificial Intelligence: Why Computers Can't Think the Way We Do,* The Belknap Press of Harvard University Press, Cambridge Mass. and London, 2021

Léger, Marc James, *Don't Network: The Avant-Garde after Networks*, Minor Compositions, Colchester, New York and Port Watson, 2018

Leibniz, Gottfried, *Philosophical Papers and Letters*, edited and introduced by L.E. Loemker, Reidel, Dordrecht, 1969

Long, Maebh ed., *The Collected Letters of Flann O'Brien*, Dalkey Archive Press, Dallas, London and Dublin, 2018

Kracauer, Siegfried, *The Salaried Masses: Duty and Distraction in Weimar Germany* [1930], translated by Quintin Hoare, with an introduction by Inka Mülder-Bach, Verso, London and New York, 1998

Mackay, Robin, Trafford, James, and Pendrell, Luke eds. *Speculative Aesthetics*, Urbanomic, Falmouth, 2014

Malm, Andreas, and the Zetkin Collective, *White Skin, Black Fuel: On the Danger of Fossil Fascism*, Verso, London and New York, 2021

Marx, Paris, *Road to Nowhere: What Silicon Valley Gets Wrong about the Future of Transportation*, Verso, London and New York, 2022

Moholy-Nagy, László, *Moholy-Nagy*, ed. Richard Kostelanetz, Documentary Monographs in Modern Art, Allen Lane, London, 1974

Nail, Thomas, *Theory of the Image*, Oxford University Press, Oxford, 2019

Negarestani, Reza, *Intelligence and Spirit*, Urbanomic, Falmouth and Sequence Press, New York, 2018

Nesbit, Molly, *Their Common Sense*, Black Dog Publishing, London, 2000

Ngai, Sianne, *Theory of the Gimmick: Aesthetic Judgment and Capitalist Form*, The Belknap Press of Harvard University Press, Cambridge Mass. and London, 2020

O'Brien, Flann (Myles na Gopaleen), *The Best of Myles: A Selection from 'Cruiskeen Lawn'*, edited and with a preface by Kevin O'Nolan, Picador, London and Sydney, 1977

O'Brien, Flann, *The Poor Mouth* [*An Béal Bocht*, 1941], translated by Patrick C. Power, illustrated by Ralph Steadman, Flamingo Modern Classic, HarperCollins, London, 1993

O'Brien, Flann, *The Third Policeman* [1940], Harper Perennial Modern Classics, HarperCollins, London, 2007

O'Brien, Flann, *At Swim-Two-Birds* [1939], Penguin Modern Classics, London, 2000

O'Connell, Micheál / Mocksim, *Contra-Invention*, Mocsim Arts/Services, Brighton, 2010

O'Connell, Micheál / Mocksim, *Less*, Mocsim Arts/Services, Brighton 2013

O'Connell, Micheál / Mocksim, *Art as 'Artificial Stupidity'*, PhD thesis, University of Sussex, 2016. Available at: http://sro.sussex.ac.uk/id/eprint/67604

O'Connell, Micheál / Mocksim, *Irish Signatures (More Pods)*, Mocsim Arts/Services, Brighton, 2019

O'Connell, Micheál / Mocksim and Madajczak, Tomasz, *NoSpace*, Mocsim Arts/Services, Brighton, 2021

O'Connell, Micheál / Mocksim, '(Bad) Faith in the Algorithm: Bureaucracy, Democracy and Tricksterism' [unpublished paper], 2021

O'Connell, Micheál / Mocksim, 'Systems Interference Art: Arguments, Samples, New Work' [unpublished paper], 2021

O'Neil, Cathy, *Weapons of Math Destruction: How Big Data Increases Inequality and Threatens Democracy*, Crown, Penguin Random House, New York, 2016

Ó Riain, Seán, *The Rise and Fall of Ireland's Celtic Tiger: Liberalism, Boom and Bust*, Cambridge University Press, Cambridge, 2014

Paglen, Trevor, *Blank Spots on the Map: The Dark Geography of the Pentagon's Secret World*, Dutton, Penguin Group, New York, 2009

Patnaik, Utsa, and Patnaik, Prabhat, *Capital and Imperialism: Theory, History, and the Present*, Monthly Review Press, New York, 2021

Peirce, Charles Sanders, *The Essential Peirce*, two volumes, ed. Peirce Edition Project, Indiana University Press, Indiana, 1992 and 1998

Ravn, Olga, *The Employees: A workplace novel of the 22nd century*, translated by Martin Aitken, Lolli Editions, London, 2020

Roberts, John, *The Necessity of Errors*, Verso, London and New York, 2011

Roberts, John, 'Dean Kenning's Kinetics', in ed. Sianne Ngai, *The Cute*, Documents of Contemporary Art, MIT Press/Whitechapel Gallery, Cambridge Mass. and London, 2022

Roden, David, *Posthuman Life: Philosophy at the Edge of the Human*, Routledge, London and New York, 2015

Ronell, Avital, *Stupidity*, University of Illinois Press, Urbana and Chicago, 2003

Rose, Gillian, *Mourning Becomes the Law: Philosophy and Representation*, Cambridge University Press, Cambridge, 1996

Steyerl, Hito, 'In Defense of the Poor Image', *e-flux journal*, No. 10, November 2009

Steyerl, Hito, 'A Sea of Data: Pattern Recognition and Corporate Animism (Forked Version)' in Clemens Apprich, Wendy Hui Kyong Chun, Florian Cramer, and Hito Steyerl, *Pattern Discrimination*, meson press, Lüneberg, and, University of Minnesota Press, Minneapolis, 2018

Stiegler, Bernard, *For a New Critique of Political Economy*, translated by Daniel Ross, Polity Press, Cambridge, 2010

Stiegler, Bernard, *The Neganthropocene*, edited, translated, and with an introduction by Daniel Ross, Open Humanities Press, London, 2018

Stiegler, Bernard, *The Age of Disruption: Technology and Madness in Computational Capitalism*, Polity Press, Cambridge, 2019

Toscano, Alberto, and Kinkle, Jeff, *Cartographies of the Absolute*, Zer0 Books, John Hunt Publishing, Alresford, Hants, 2014

Žižek, Slavoj, *Hegel in a Wired Brain*, Bloomsbury Academic, London, 2020

Zupančič, Alenka, *The Odd One In: On Comedy*, MIT Press, Cambridge Mass. and London, 2008

Zylinska, Joanna, *AI Art: Machine Visions and Warped Dreams*, Open Humanities Press, London, 2020

www.ingramcontent.com/pod-product-compliance
Lightning Source LLC
Chambersburg PA
CBHW070216190526
45161CB00005B/269/J
*9781904354390*